Remember When...?

Remember When...?

Family, Friends, and Recipes

By
Clara Belle Hooks Eschmann

Mercer University Press
Macon, Georgia

©Mercer University Press
6316 Peake Road
Macon, Georgia 31210
1998

Library of Congress Cataloging-in-Publication Data

Eschmann, Clara.
Remember When?—: family, friends, and recipes / Clara
Belle Hooks Eschmann.
p. cm.
ISBN 0-86554-623-1 (alk. paper)
1. Cookery, American. 2. Georgia—Social life and cus-
toms—Anecdotes. I. Title.
TX715.E717   1998
641.5973—dc21
98-38042
CIP

Table of Contents

Dedication

I would like to dedicate this book to my parents, William Glenn and Clara Belle Davenport Hooks and to my older sister, Leila Davenport Hooks McConnell, whose love and tender care of me, through the years, I consider to be one of my greatest blessings.

Had it not been for *The Macon Telegraph* this book might never have come into existence. For approximately twenty years I served as food editor for this publication and after retirement from that work I continued to compose a weekly column of recipes. Eventually my superiors approached me about writing on my past experiences. The end result was Remember When...?, which has now been running in the paper each Wednesday for over two years.

I had thought that I might like to write about my growing-up years especially for my children and grandchildren. There never seemed to be time so I am now happy to have made an entry into this filed by way of the newspaper. I was delighted that Mercer University Press offered to publish this book.

Children today are growing up in such a sophisticated, hi-tech world that I felt they should know how their elders grew and developed. As youngsters we used our imaginations, played simple games and had great fun in such a gentle manner that I'm sure it all must seem peculiar to the younger ones today.

I'm very grateful to the numerous readers who were kind enough to phone, write or stop me on the streets to say that they liked this new column. I'd constantly been urged through Straight Talk inserts in the *Telegraph* to make a book of these almost forgotten times. This helped me to know that the appeal seemed widespread.

Many could orient with what I had to tell and others found it amusing. Some of my young friends even said that they were teaching lots of these ideas to their children. Consequently it seems that those of us who remember these days still have something to offer our youngsters.

I was glad to be told that I could include some of my favorite, family recipes in this new work. The research on these has been a delight. I'm glad that my mother and maternal grandmother kept such good files. It's a pleasure for me to even see their handwriting again and also to use many of these good dishes.

There are numerous persons who helped me with the preparation for this book. Foremost is Bill Weaver, research editor for *The Macon Telegraph*. He quietly and quickly pulled the necessary material from our own files for me.

Carol Hudler, publisher, and Cecil Bentley, executive editor, were behind this publication from the start. The two librarians, R. J. Petrovick and Harriet Comer are always ready and eager to help any of us with research needs. Encouragement was given by many of my young friends at our office which I greatly appreciate. Ed Grisamore, who published through the same press some of his columns last year in *True Gris*, provided valuable information in short cuts for making the material ready for use.

My daughter, Clare Eschmann Fisher, made a trip from her home in Nashville, Tennessee, to help me proof-read the entire book. She even poured over it a second time for the final reading. Scores of friends carefully read for mistakes including two of the people who are often mentioned in this book Martha Marshall Dykes, Americus, and Elizabeth Mathis Cheatham, Atlanta. They spent a day in Macon with me pouring over these contents. My son, Ed Eschmann, Dawson, also offered extended assistance.

Local readers included: Cora Wayne Wright, Carrie Popper Becker, Joyce Hudson, Emmy Lou Goff, Marie Wilson, Betty Alexander Smith, and Mary Coates. Their diligence and eagerness to assist in accuracy is greatly appreciated.

While only fifty of the earlier columns are included in this publication I hope that they will bring pleasure.

These were selected according to response from readers. I will forever relish the friends who said, "When are you ever going to put to your columns into a book?" God bless you, and many thanks for your votes of confidence. Now join me in an opportunity to Remember When...?

Fall

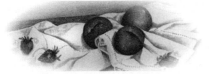 *School Reopens*

After the public swimming pool closed for the Summer, it wasn't long before school would be opening.

I don't recall that it was as early as they begin now. Of course we didn't have snowstorms in that part of the state very often. Consequently, there were no plans for closing except for holidays.

Most of us got new dresses and shoes for the first day of school. The most popular footwear featured little brown oxfords or short laced shoes. These didn't show dirt, were leather, and could be polished when grubby. They were very serviceable. If our Sunday shoes were black patents and getting small, we were allowed to wear them to classes sometimes until we outgrew them.

Mama and Grandmother Davenport made our new outfits for my sister, Leila, and me. Other mothers sewed for their children, too. We always had bloomers or gathered underpants to match. The latter had elastic at the waist and around the thighs and were made of the same material as the outer garment. We tried to find high-topped socks to match these new clothes. They usually had a cuff on the top that was sometimes patterned, or it could be just plain.

There was usually an excursion for purchasing our new book satchels. These were made of canvas and had pockets on the outside and matching leather straps that latched them. They were carried by firm handles of the same material as the straps.

Our books were furnished for all classes, but we transported them to our houses for homework. We were expected to supply writing tablets, pencils, crayons and, later, watercolor boxes for art classes. These we carried on the first day of school in our new bags.

A majority of the students had wooden pencil boxes for our writing equipment that could be kept in our school desks. We often wrote our names on them in case they disappeared. They could be transported in our satchels if we preferred. We also acquired new, large erasers for the beginning of each year.

Shopping for all of this was fun. The items were generally purchased at the S.H. Kress Co., our local 5-and-10-cent store. We spoke of it always as "Kresses." It would be fun if I could remember the prices of the above items. I'll bet it would be astonishing this day and time.

With all of the summer fun behind, we immediately began anticipating our new school year. My friend, Martha, and I began praying that we would be in the same classroom and also with the teacher of our choice. We were never disappointed.

Martha was almost a year younger than I and could not start to school in the first grade with me since Sept. 1 was the cutoff date. When "Aunt" Mattie, her mother, found that she could begin classes in Quitman, the town of my friend's maternal grandmother, and transfer to Americus after her November birthday, she was sent there for starting school. This was joy for both of us to be able to continue together through our school days in Americus.

The first day back to school was always exciting. The girls would gather on our side of the school in the playground. We would look over each other's new outfits and school equipment. Most likely we arrived early on that day in order to see everybody again. Many of our classmates lived across town from us, and we saw them only occasionally until classes began again.

As I best recall, the first day back was not a full one. We lined up and marched into Furlow Grammar to the piano playing of our music teacher, the late Mrs. R.J. Maynard.

Usually the two classes for each grade were directly across from each other or right next door. Consequently, all of the children in the various grades would collect between their two rooms out in the hall. The two teachers would be there, too, and announce to us which room would be theirs.

Then came the real excitement. Students' names would be called alphabetically for each by the teachers. My last name being Hooks, I would be announced before Martha, whose last name was Marshall. We would look hopefully at each other prior to my entering the classroom. When she marched in also, we were both thrilled. It just would not have been fair for us to be separated.

Desks would be assigned, and our books distributed. There was also a "cloak closet" at the end of each class room. It contained hooks for hanging our coats or umbrellas. We were designated our own spots. There were no lockers. We could hang our lunch boxes under the coats or just place them on the floor beneath.

This area was used to separate naughty children from the class for brief periods of time, also. I can remember hurrying in and out as if I had been trapped there for some misdeed. However, it was a very functional area for our personal clothing.

We could hardly wait to get home and tell our parents about the new teacher, the friends who were in our classroom and what interesting things had happened on the first day of a new school year. I wonder if children today enjoy school as much as we did.

Mama always had something extra special for our supper on that big day. The following recipe was a favorite and seemed very festive.

Macaroni Mousse Ring

1 1/2 cups scalded milk
1/4 cup melted butter
3 eggs, well beaten
1 pimiento, chopped fine
1 cup cooked elbow macaroni, about 3/4 cup uncooked
1 sweet green pepper, diced
1 tablespoon onion, diced
1/2 teaspoon salt
1 tablespoon Worcestershire sauce
1 cup soft bread crumbs
1/2 cup sharp cheese, grated
1/2 cup sliced mushrooms

Scald milk and add butter, mixing until melted. Slowly add remaining ingredients in the order given, reserving 1/2 cup of bread crumbs. Pour into a buttered ring mold, top with remaining bread crumbs. Bake for 40 minutes in a pan of hot water in an oven registering 350 degrees. When done, remove from oven, allow to set about 5 minutes, turn onto platter and fill with creamed chicken, turkey, ham, mushrooms or meat of your choice. We sometimes used green peas and carrots, well drained, for the center. Ring serves 6 to 8. Easy to make and so pretty!

Pear Relish

1 peck of hard, sugar pears, ground
6 cups sugar
6 cups cider vinegar
1 teaspoon celery seed
1 teaspoon whole cloves
2 teaspoons salt
3 sweet red peppers, ground
4 green bell peppers, ground
3 large onions, ground

Wash and drain all vegetables and pears well before grinding. Mix sugar and vinegar. Bring to a boil and add remaining ingredients. Cook slowly and stir frequently until thick. Pour into sterilized jars and seal.

Our young lady neighbor, Georgia Lumpkin, who lived next door was a real beauty. She was popular, too, and my sister and I observed many young friends calling for her to go out with them. She lived with her aunt Lily. Her mother had died when she was born and this wonderful relative reared her.

Before she returned to college each year, she hosted a dancing party on the front porch of their house. My sister, Leila, and I were almost always invited to serve punch to the guests and also to wind and attend to the Victrola.

In those days there were no tape players. Nor were there electrically operated record players that could be stacked with recordings that dropped automatically.

We would dress in our Sunday best and go over in advance of the guests. Georgia, our older friend, would show us the stack of records and pick out a few to put on top since she knew which ones were most desired. We were cautioned to be very careful with them since they were breakable.

In addition to the punch bowl, there would be a bounty of sweet treats. We Hooks girls handled serving these as well. We were also to tell "Aunt" Lily when to replenish both the beverage and sweets.

As the guests arrived, we were awed by their clothes. My sister enjoyed seeing the latest styles since she was almost a teen-ager and those attending were only a few years older than she. I remember seeing very short skirts on the women. Some were pleated, and others were tight and split on each side, but not high like we see them today.

The tops were sleeveless with a wide band across the shoulders. The necklines were not extremely low. This would have been in the late '20s, so maybe you are familiar with what I was viewing.

Some of the females wore headbands with an ostrich feather at the back. Others pinned flowers into their curls or ribbons. Their necklaces were usually ropes of beads.

I didn't pay much attention to the men's fashions. They usually came in large hats, which were removed upon arrival, and their suits were light colored. Some wore white jackets and dark or striped pants.

All were very polite to us two young neighborhood girls. They would come over for a cup of punch and seem most appreciative when we served them. They also thanked us when we could supply their musical requests.

Since my sister was several years older, she could wind the Victrola better than I, but I took turns as well. As best I remember, it would play one or two records before slowly winding down. Then our work began again. Leila also handled most of the fragile records.

Needles had to be changed on this type machine, too. We were not allowed to do that, but our neighbor-hostess would recognize the scratching of an old one and fix it herself.

We were fascinated with the dancing. It was in the era of the Charleston, the Black Bottom and the Flea Hop. When a few of the guests saw us patting our feet in time with the music, they suggested that we try dancing, too. Leila was prompt to the call, but I was timid. However, once she got into it and did so well, I tried, too. I found the Flea Hop easy and everybody stood around and cheered me. Eventually I caught on to the other popular steps. Our efforts must have seemed ridiculous to those older dancers.

These entertainments were given on the porch of the house because it was still very hot weather in Americus during the early fall. There were two large swings on the porch and the dancers would often stop for a brief period and enjoy the breezes created by swinging. Many of the females carried little folding feather or ivory hand fans. They were in constant use.

Lots of times a male and female guest would walk off the porch and into the dark part of the yard. Naive as I was, I remember asking Leila why in the world were they not dancing or swinging? She got very close to my ear and whispered, "I think they must be kissing."

Horrors! I couldn't possibly imagine such a thing. These were people kissing and they weren't even kin to each other. It made no sense to me at that tender age.

The dances usually began around 8 P.M. and lasted a couple of hours. Often the guests would pile into cars when the party concluded, and ride around town a while. There would be much scrambling about who was to ride in which car. They seemed to enjoy grouping into as few vehicles as possible.

My sister and I would then help take the punch cups to the kitchen of our neighbor's house. We'd stack the records and move the arm of the Victrola from its playing position to the rest that held it on one side. We would then close it and return home.

I can remember hearing some of the cars return from their rides after I was in my bed. Often there would be singing among the group, but the engines of that day made enough noise to announce their return without the help of songs. Of course, the following days, Leila and I would teach the girls on our street the new dance steps we had learned. We'd all seen them in movies but never tried them before.

I hope you enjoy this recipe for a wonderful, refreshing drink as well as the cookie one.

Americus Fruit Punch

2 quarts boiling water
4 tea bags
Juice of 4 lemons
2 quarts pineapple juice
3 cups sugar
2 cups freshly squeezed orange juice
2 quarts ginger ale
Maraschino cherries, juice included, and orange slices for garnishing
Large block of ice

Boil water and add tea bags. Allow to steep 10 minutes. Remove and add sugar and juices. Chill. Place a large block of ice in center of punch bowl. Pour over punch and lastly add ginger ale. Float orange slices and cherries if desired. Makes about 2 gallons. Crushed mint leaves may be added to hot tea and removed along with tea bags. This offers added flavor. Makes about 40 servings.

Peppermint Crisps

1/4 cup shortening
1/2 cup sugar
1 cup all-purpose flour, unsifted
1/2 teaspoon baking powder
1/4 teaspoon soda
1/4 teaspoon salt
1/4 teaspoon nutmeg
1 well beaten egg
1 tablespoon milk
3 to 4 tablespoons crushed peppermint stick candy, or to taste

Cream shortening and sugar. Sift dry ingredients together, including spice. Add to first mixture alternating with milk and beaten egg, which have been previously combined.

Blend well. Drop by teaspoon about 2 inches apart onto greased cookie sheet or sheets. Flatten cookies by pressing with a glass dipped in flour. Sprinkle each cookie with candy and gently press it into the dough. Bake at 350 degrees for 12 minutes. Cool slightly before removing from pans. Store in airtight containers. after completely cool. (Using extra candy in this recipe doesn't change the texture. I prefer 4 tablespoons but then I like peppermint!) Makes 4 to 5 dozen cookies.

Note On Tombstone

Can your believe that one of the most fun things my friend Martha and I did in our youth was to walk out to Oak Grove Cemetery in Americus and read the inscriptions? Sounds dreary, I know, but we thought it was fun and some of the writings were hilarious.

We generally made these journeys on a Sunday afternoon in cool weather, spring, fall or warm winter days. After church and a big meal in our separate homes, we'd take our stroll. There were several routes to follow, and we enjoyed taking different ones. They were all about the same walking distance.

Once we entered the main gates at Oak Grove it was necessary to find our favorite inscription and the accompanying write-in that somebody had scribbled beneath it. This was located in the old part of the cemetery, close to the front. We knew exactly how to find it and generally started our visits at this spot. I don't recall knowing whose grave it was, but the epitaph read:

"Dear passer-by / As you are now, / So once was I.
As I am now, / So shall you be, / Prepare yourself
To follow me."
The hand-written note beneath read:
"To follow you / I'm not content,
For I know not / Which way you went."

Giggles and laughter literally bent us double after each reading. I have been told that this message has been in book collections from other cemeteries. I don't know just where. But it was certainly in our town's burial ground. I'm sure, in this day and time, that the hand-written message has weathered away or been rubbed off, but it was truly in evidence when I was a young girl. It never failed to amuse us, and I'm sure others as well in Americus.

After our first stop I would usually take my friend to view the many family graves on all four sides of my ancestors. Martha's grandparents had come from Quitman and Cedartown, so she just adopted my relatives on these journeys.

All four sets of my great-grandparents are buried there. That seems like one for the *Guiness Book of Records*. Obviously all of my family loved the area through the years and never moved away. There were also many great-aunts, -uncles and old friends, whom we both knew, resting in that great spot.

In addition, there is a small Confederate graveyard that we never failed to see. The small markers seemed so regular in their placing. We looked for names that seemed familiar, but I don't recall finding any.

Our precious second-grade school teacher, Miss Genevieve Morgan, died a few years after we were in her class. We adored her and often took flowers for her grave. I would also take them to the headstone of my paternal grandmother, who died at age 26. Of course, I never knew Leila Shepherd Hooks, but my father and his two brothers spoke of her so lovingly that I felt as if I knew her.

There is also a little fountain in the cemetery. It was always well-kept and if the day seemed warm enough, we were likely to take off our shoes and socks and wade around the edges. Drying our feet was a bit of a problem, but shaking them hard and fanning them with our skirts seemed to work well.

If we decided not to stay for a long period, we were likely to stop by and see my Davenport grandparents, who lived between our house and the cemetery. This was always good for an afternoon snack and a great welcome on their part for our unexpected visits.

Sometimes we would see school friends from that part of town and visited with them if time permitted. All of this seems a strange pleasure for young girls, but it was a joy that never diminished for Martha and me. We laugh about it a lot now, always with fun reminiscences.

Today I am offering recipes typical of our big Sunday dinners. These were especially popular on cool or winter days. I can't believe that they are unique in this part of the world, but I recall them with genuine delight.

Lemon-Parsley-Chicken Casserole

2 cups cold boiled rice
1 1/2 cups minced, cooked chicken
3 tablespoons chicken broth
1 tablespoon chopped fresh parsley
1/2 teaspoon grated lemon rind
Salt and pepper to taste
Cream sauce or gravy for topping

Grease a plain mold or casserole dish and line throughout with rice, pressing it with a spoon to make sure it clings. Add the parsley, lemon rind, salt, pepper and broth to chicken. Fill the center of rice lining with the seasoned chicken. Cover with a little additional rice. Put on a lid and steam for 3/4 of an hour in 250 degree oven. Cool slightly before turning out on a hot dish. Top with gravy or cream sauce. Serves 6.

Scalloped Eggplant

1 medium eggplant
Salted water for boiling eggplant
1 or 2 onions
2 tablespoons butter
1 teaspoon Worcestershire sauce
1 egg
Salt and pepper to taste
Cracker crumbs

Peel and cut eggplant in large pieces. Let stand in cold water for about half and hour. Drain and add one or two onions, chopped, to eggplant. Place in water enough to half cover vegetables. Cook until tender and most of water has been absorbed. Drain if necessary. Mash well with butter. Add Worcestershire and beaten egg. Season with salt and pepper to taste. Place in buttered baking dish and top with buttered cracker crumbs.Bake for about 30 minutes or until lightly brown on top. Serves 6.

Memories Toted In Lunchbox

Every time I see a big, yellow school bus filled with children my heart sinks for them. I feel the same way about car pools, and believe me I had my share of those. There are eleven years between my oldest and youngest children and I felt I was on duty for eons. Why do I feel sad for today's children? Because I remember the fun we had walking to school with neighborhood friends. No, I didn't walk three or four miles in the cold to a little red school house. Mine was only three long blocks from my door. And if it was a stormy day we were driven to our classes.

Our street was a short one and all the children were friends. The older ones took care of the younger and helped them at the two streets we had to cross. We also walked home together, talking about the day's events and planning our afternoon free time.

One of the best things we did was make a game of kicking a rock as we walked. We would see who could kick the farthest and also who could reach school first with the rock.

You had to have a flat stone because uneven ones rolled too easily. When a good rock was found, it was carefully guarded for continuous use. It would be pocketed at school and put in a dresser drawer on returning home. The same rock was most helpful in playing hop scotch. Kicking a stone was not a daily event, but done often enough to be fun and not boring. Naturally we had to play on pleasant days.

Our innocent walk, with feet kicking, took a little more time than just going the distance from home to school. But it was such fun. Of course, we took turns and had to wait for each kicker to perform before going forward. Should we accidently kick it into grass, that was tough, and if it went into the street the player had to go back to the starting point and wait for another turn.

If we heard the first school bell before reaching our destination we simply picked up our prize stone and ran the rest of the way. The winner was the person who was ahead.

With all this activity we were juggling our little lunch boxes and holding onto books as well. We did not have lunch rooms and since we started school at 8:30 A.M. and were out at 2 P.M., our mothers felt we needed a healthy snack in the two recess periods.

The midday meal was saved for my sister and me on divided plates in the warming oven of the old wood stove. We enjoyed it together when we returned home. Our school snack was most often fruit with a few crackers. Sometimes we had special treats like mother's Cheese Cookies or Oatmeal and Raisin Bars.

During sugar cane season my father would cut enough wedges for both of his girls to fill our little tin boxes. They were lined with waxed paper and the lids tightly closed. Mine was blue and Leila's pink. They had two handles that came up over the top.

My closest friend, Martha, and I always shared our lunches. Our mothers were the closest of friends and had the same principles about healthy snacks. Some classmates in Americus still tease us about how we would split our apples into halves, if that's what we'd both brought, in order to have the same.

I was delighted when her mom sent Date Nut Bread and she was equally pleased with our Cheese Cookies. If things did not come out evenly, we simply broke them in halves to be sure neither had more than the other.

School lunch programs today are more than we had in my early years. Many of the schools have menu choices. Imagine! I've eaten in many school cafeterias and never had a bad meal. But I still like to think about my little blue tin lunch box. I wish I still had it.

Aunt Mattie's Date Nut Bread

1 cup dates, chopped
1 cup milk
3/4 cup sugar
2 cups whole wheat flour
1/2 teaspoon salt
3 teaspoons baking powder
1 cup pecans, chopped

Dust dates and nuts with some of the flour. Sift remaining flour, salt and baking powder together. Add sugar and blend in milk. Fold dates and nuts into mixture blending well. Pour into greased and floured loaf pan. Bake at 350 degrees 35 to 45 minutes. Test with cake tester for doneness. Bread should draw from sides of pan and be slightly brown and dry on top when done.

Mama's Sharp Cheese Cookies

1 cup sifted flour
1 teaspoon salt
1/2 cup butter or margarine
1 cup grated sharp cheese
1/2 teaspoon paprika
Dash of cayenne
3 1/2 tablespoons cold water
Pecan halves or cinnamon and sugar for topping

Sift flour and salt together. Add butter and cheese, both at room temperature. Cut well into flour, mixing thoroughly. Add paprika and cayenne blending well into dough. Add water last. Roll dough 1/4-inch thick on floured board. Cut into rounds or desired shapes. Top with pecan half or a light sprinkling of sugar before baking.

Bake in 350 degree oven, on greased cookie sheets, for 10 to 12 minutes. Cookies should be lightly brown on tops. Remove while hot and cool. Store in air tight containers. Makes 4 to 5 dozen round cookies 1 1/2 to 2-inch size.

Haircut
A Close Shave

Getting haircuts was an essential part of my growing up. Most of the little girls my age wore the same style with bangs. Mama insisted that my side hair should be trimmed so that the tips of my ear lobes just showed. The backs were what we called "shingled" or cropped very close in a curved page boy. Then our necks were shaved up to the hair line.

We did not go to a hair dresser or beauty shop. The late Mrs. L.B. Garner had the only beauty salon in Americus during my growing-up years there. The older girls and women went to her, but not Leila, who was lucky enough to get the curls in our family and wore her wavy hair in a different style. But she also went to the same hair person the children used.

My friend Martha and I had identical haircuts. We all went to the barber shop on the alley side of the old Windsor Hotel. I can still see that red, white, and blue barber pole turning as we walked in for cuts.

We always went to a Mr. Elder. There were two other barbers but I have forgotten their names. Sometimes Martha and I would flip a coin or draw straws to see who would go first. The other would sit in a chair and watch.

Since we lived only a half mile from the center of town, the two of us were allowed to go together to the barber's. During school sessions we usually went on a Saturday. Our mothers decided when they thought we looked shabby.

We generally made an excursion with a trio of stops: the barber shop, the 5-and-10, and the drug store. The last stop meant a nickel ice cream cone—our treat for the day.

She and I were together recently and neither of us could remember biting into the scoop of ice cream. We always licked it to make it last the entire way back home. If it began dripping on our hands, we had to push the contents way down into the cone with our tongues. Of course, we took care of what was on our hands with a general swipe of the mouth.

This was before there were double dips of ice cream. And I can also remember well when those delicious wafer-type cones came our way. By that time, the price had risen to 10 cents. Imagine such inflation! Recently Martha and I paid $2.25 for two dips. It hurt our feelings. And yes, we licked ours just as before.

But, back to the barber shop. Mr. Elder draped us well with a large cloth that fell way over our knees. This caught most of the cut hair. I can remember squeezing my eyes closed when he got to the bangs. They tickled as the trimmings fell over my face.

Once he was finished, he would whirl the chair around to let me view my new style in a large mirror. He always cut with us facing out into the shop. He had a large brush-type duster that he sprinkled well with talcum powder. He would dust us across the backs of our necks and sometimes under the chin if the trimming had been a wild one. It was a very refreshing and pleasant smelling finale.

Martha recalled the day that we were asked to take her younger brother, Tom, to the shop with us. Being older, we naturally put him third in line to get the treatment. One of us sat with him while the other was being cut.

When we were through, we told Mr. Elder and Tom that we were going to "run over to the 5-and-10" for a few minutes. It was only around the corner, so we asked Mr. Elder to please keep Tom in the chair until we returned. We promised to hurry.

Neither of us can recall if we stayed longer than expected, or just what happened. We certainly misjudged our time. When we got back and looked at poor little Tom, he was practically a skin head. Both of us nearly fainted though he seemed quite unaware of his new hair style. We were furious with Mr. Elder. It's much nicer to blame somebody else.

All of us got the standard ice cream. She and I sort of choked ours down because we were so disturbed about Tom's hair.

"What in the world can I tell Mama?" my friend worried. We tried to think up all sorts of fancy tales. There was nothing to do but speak the truth. We had to sort of whisper in order not to reveal our fears to the newest shaved head on the block.

I went home with her to face the grim look and chewing out that was deserved. After all, I had certainly been a part of the deal. I well remember

"Aunt" Mattie's shocked face as she said, "Why in the world did you girls let this go so far? I can hardly recognize my child."

This astonished previously unaware Tom to such an extent that he began to sob and so did we. How very ashamed my friend and I were over such an experience.

We all decided that at least his hair wouldn't have to be cut again soon. And it would grow out again, we knew. But all of that was little consolation at the time.

I'm sure that we made repeated trips to the barber shop with Tom, but we never left him alone again while we journeyed off for our own pleasures. It was a good lesson in taking care of a younger person. We were given a few cookies to smooth over the days' events. The recipes follow.

Easy Brownies

1 stick butter
1 cup sugar
2 eggs
1/2 cup flour
2 squares melted bitter or milk chocolate
1 cup chopped pecans
Pinch of salt

Cream butter and sugar. Add eggs and beat well. Add flour and salt and mix thoroughly. Melt chocolate and combine to mixture along with pecans. Bake in greased, square cake pan for 25 minutes at 350 degrees. Cut in squares when cool and store in air-tight containers.

Peanut Butter Cookies

1 cup brown sugar
1 cup white sugar
1 cup peanut butter
1 cup butter
2 eggs
3 cups plain flour
1 teaspoon soda
1/2 teaspoon salt
1 teaspoon baking powder
1/2 cup milk, if needed to thin dough

Cream butters with sugar and mix well. Beat eggs and add. Sift flour, soda, salt and baking powder; combine two mixtures. If dough becomes too stiff to handle, add enough milk to thin it. Chill and make into small balls. Place on greased cookie sheets, 2 inches apart. Flatten with fork dipped in sugar. Bake in moderate oven, 350 degrees, for 12 minutes.

Trips In a Model T

Today I'd like to tell you what I remember about various automobiles of my day. Daddy had a Model-T Ford, as did most farmers in our area. Wagons with mules, not trucks, were used for hauling materials to and from the farms. Our car was mostly for transportation, but it certainly took us to the peach orchards often. The vehicle would give us a bumpy ride over plowed ruts in the fields while plants were checked by our father. Daddy often spoke of our car as a "flivver," a term that I heard others use in that day.

Our car was a two-seater, open front and back, and featured a running board across the two sides that ended in hood-type fenders over the front and back wheels. Most of the cars were alike in this respect, even if they were different models. The children all liked to hop on the running boards for short drives into the garage or just down the street. We'd step up on it and hold tightly to the door sides of the car. This was easy since there were no windows to be opened.

When it rained, there were isinglass windows encased in heavy, black, oil-coated canvas (to match the color of our car.) These were portable and stored in the trunk of the auto behind the spare wheel that stuck up on the back.

Driving had to be very slow and careful when we were enclosed during rains. But the coverings served their purpose in keeping us dry and allowing some side visibility.

My uncle Quimby Melton always had nicer, enclosed cars. His were used mostly for pleasure and in-town driving. He first had an Essex and later a larger vehicle that was a Hudson. Even though they came with roll up windows, they also featured running boards and a spare tire on the rear.

No matter what kind of car was owned, most of them stalled often, and many were so slow starting that they had to be cranked off in order to run. Numerous arms were broken when the hard metal jack was used and flipped back too quickly to remove the person's hand.

This jack was attached in the front under the center of the car hood. The auto had to be left in idle and fully braked while the hand-turning began. If the person starting the car was not quick about removing his arm, once the engine began the heavy, z-shaped attachment would flip around so quickly that it could hit a forearm with such force that a break was inevitable.

Once the motor started, the driver had to quickly jump into place and press the accelerator to keep the car going. I well remember how Mama always cautioned Daddy to be careful when it was his misfortune to resort to these measures. He never had a break, but I recall many who did.

Before I was born my Grandfather (Thomas Barden) Hooks, had an electric car. I don't know that I ever saw it, but it was certainly the town talk for many years. As a farmer himself, he eventually resorted to the same type of car everyone had.

Probably the finest car that I recall as a child was owned by an older relative whom we called "Aunt" Clay. She was very "well-to-do" and lived across the street from my maternal Davenport grandparents. She was a good friend to them and also to my little family. She was an elegant lady.

I believe that her car was a Packard. I know that it was an extremely expensive and fancy automobile. The best part to me was that it had been equipped with little, pull-out back seats that were in front of the regular long rear one. They were designed for extra passengers in the long vehicle.

There were also tiny crystal vases attached to the interior sides of the car between the front and back area. They were often filled with seasonal flowers. I well remember these unique features, which would naturally attract a child. The car was large and black. In fact, just about all cars were that one color, although I do remember a few cream colored cars, especially when roadsters came into our lives.

On drives with "Aunt" Clay, Leila and I sat on the pull-out seats. Though we quietly endured these trips with our elders, we felt "set up" just to be riding in such style. We always hoped to see some friends to whom we could wave just to show off our elegant setting.

My children will truly laugh unceasingly if they have an opportunity to read this recollection. They know how poorly informed I am about present day automobiles. I really don't know one make from another.

When they happen to ask me about what sort of car a friend drives, I usually reply that it's blue, white, green, or whatever. Consequently, I may be quite misinformed about the above, but I feel very certain about the Fords of that day and the Melton cars. All were a special part of my young life.

Here are dandy little recipes from one of Mama's old books.

Apple Puffs

1 cup flour
1/2 cup sugar
3 apples
1 egg
1/2 level teaspoon baking powder
2/3 cup milk
Pinch of salt
Hot fat for frying

Sift together flour, salt and baking powder. Add sugar and apples that have been peeled, cored and chopped well. Mix in a rather stiff batter with the egg and milk. Drop by spoonful into hot fat and cook until the puffs are golden brown and the apples tender. Drain on soft paper and serve hot with a dessert sauce, if desired. Or you may prefer to coat with powdered sugar.

Onion Custard Pie

2 cups chopped onions
6 slices bacon
2 cups milk
3 eggs
1/2 cup grated sharp cheese or powdered Parmesan cheese
1/2 cup cracker crumbs

Chop onions. Cook bacon until crisp and crumble. Cook onions in bacon drippings until tender. Mix eggs and milk and add to onions and crumbled bacon along with any drippings remaining. Put in casserole dish and top with cheese and bread crumbs. Bake at 350 degrees until brown. Serves 8.

Childhood Club

In little towns, like Americus where I grew up, young people were reliant on each other and their families for entertainment. There were no televisions but we did attend the movies every Saturday afternoon. There was always a running serial that we dared not miss. New ones followed the old once they came to a conclusion. This was in addition to the regular show.

We stopped by the corner drug store and bought an ice cream cone for a nickel. The movie was the costly price of a dime.

Radios were prevalent but were only allowed to be used in my home after my sister Leila and I had completed our homework. This meant weekend listening with the family or friends, most of whom had the same regulations as ours. Actually, after lessons were completed, we often preferred playing a family game or being read to by our father.

Board and card games were very popular with most of us. Our daddy always felt it was good for us to play and learn how to be good losers and not boastful winners. I distinctly recall weeping bitterly when I first started playing if I were not the winner. I didn't much mind falling behind with my parents, but my older sister just had no business at all beating me. Bless her heart, she has always been so kind and gentle and was the first to try to console me if she had been victorious. But I was tearful for many losses.

Eventually Daddy's theory worked well and it paid off considerably when I was away from home and playing with friends. Parcheesi and bingo were particularly important to all of us and actually taught us a little about numbers and some arithmetic, which didn't hurt a soul. Card games were soon introduced beginning with go fishing, set back, hearts, casino, cribbage, double solitaire, patience, and eventually bridge. Since there were four members in my family, we were ideal for most of the board and card games.

When we were first taught bridge, I recall Daddy would bring home a little prize for the high scorer each weekend night except Sunday. It was always candy or cookies or something that could be shared, but the top scorer was the one who opened the treat and passed it to the rest of the family. Cards were strictly forbidden in my staunch Methodist home on the Sabbath.

We played auction bridge, certainly nothing like the newer more complicated game that we know today. It was much easier but a good lead into contract that is now so popular. One of the unique things that I recall about this game was "aces being easy." This was when both competitors had two aces each and were equally awarded 20 points on their scores.

Most of our friends learned this game too, since our mothers played often and taught us. A group of us, ages eleven and twelve, decided to have our own bridge club. Of course, we had to solicit the approval of our mothers, since we expected to serve refreshments, the same as they did for their own similar events. We met on Friday afternoons, after school, and each hostess was responsible for the high and low (booby was what we called it) prize. The hostess' mother always had lovely treats for us. In the summer it might have been ice cream and cake along with salted pecans and iced tea, but after school hours we usually had a light salad plate with finger sandwiches and lemonade or fruit juice for a beverage. Cokes were not prevalent in those days.

All our mothers seemed pleased to back our effort. They were glad for us to learn to be nice hostesses and offered encouragement. I distinctly recall my mother calling me into an adjoining room when the club was meeting with me, to tell me that I should lower a shade on a facing window that was hard on the eyes of some of my guests with the afternoon sun pouring into the room. She was gentle and would never have suggested this to me in front of the others. But she said, "You must always be sure that your guests are comfortable in every respect." It was a valuable lesson and one that has followed me through life.

Our two tables of bridge sometimes grew to three if we decided to invite other friends. But what I consider most amazing is that the little club, started so many years ago, is still in existence in my home town. It is now reduced to only one table. There are three original members who still attend. It is no longer held weekly but just once a month. My darling friend, the late Susan Myrick, was so intrigued by our childhood bridge club that she urged me to write about it for some magazine. At that time there were still six original members living in Americus and continuing our childhood club. Some have died but many are still alive and living in other towns.

We all realize that our earliest game taught us much about the more complicated one and still relish the thoughts of that weekly meeting with close friends. We truly learned good lessons and had a most enjoyable time.

Following are recipes that Mother had for me sometimes when I was the hostess. They seem more like warm weather foods, but when we lose our home-grown tomatoes perhaps the aspic is a good fill-in salad for cooler months as well. This was a favorite of mine and Mother used to serve it with finger sandwiches when we hosted the party.

Tomato Aspic

1 quart tomato or tomato-vegetable juice
1 tablespoon vinegar
2 tablespoons fresh lemon juice
1 tablespoon salt
1/2 teaspoon cayenne pepper
1/2 cup cold water
4 envelopes plain gelatin
4 ribs celery, chopped
1 (5-ounce) bottle olives, chopped
1 tablespoon grated onion
1 medium size bell pepper, chopped (optional)

Heat tomato juice to boiling point. Add all seasonings. Dissolve gelatin in cold water then add to the hot mixture, stirring vigorously in order to dissolve completely. Allow to cool to the thickness of egg whites and add chopped vegetables, mixing well.

Pour into individual molds or one ring mold. Any used should be lightly greased with salad oil or mayonnaise. This enables unmolding much easier. Chill until completely firm. Unmold onto bed of lettuce and top with mayonnaise. Serves 10 to 18.

Homemade Mayonnaise

3 egg yolks
Juice of half a lemon or more, as desired for flavor
1 pint vegetable oil
1 1/2 teaspoons salt, or to taste
Dash of cayenne pepper

In a bowl or mixer container, put egg yolks. Beat them well then add half of the lemon juice and mix; this gives a thin mixture. Take one cup of the oil and pour in a fourth of it at the time, very slowly, stirring or beating constantly. Add remaining cup of oil less slowly beating constantly. Next add lemon juice, salt and pepper, beating well. Now add second cup of oil, pouring in rapidly and beating constantly. The dressing should be stiff enough to hold its shape. Put into an air tight container, cover tightly and refrigerate. Keeps up to 10 days refrigerated. Makes 1 pint.

It's strange that Halloween today is almost a turn back to the way it was when I was a child. I mean by that the trick and treating my children enjoyed was not a part of my childhood. It appears, with so many unfortunate problems on the streets now, it will soon be obsolete for today's youngsters.

I hope my observation is incorrect, for I know what joy our children had visiting homes in the neighborhood on that scary night. Their return home with bags full of candies and homemade goodies was pleasure for us all to see and hear about. They traveled with friends and visited up and down streets near our house.

Perhaps there are some areas where this tradition still exists. In my own area of Shirley Hills, we meet at a public park off Nottingham Drive for a hot dog roast. Older people, like I, take treats to the children there and have an opportunity to admire their costumes. We visit with neighbors and have a thoroughly good, short party time.

Some of the older children go treat calling after the party, but only in our own neighborhood and always with two or more adults. This makes for safety. They can no longer roam the area with hopes of completely filling their bags as my children did. These chaperoned tricksters go to designated streets and for a brief time, especially if it's a school night. I congratulate the parents who devised this wise annual plan.

When I was little, there were no treats handed out as my friends and I strolled around on our short street. We simply dressed up mostly in sheets to appear as ghosts, or wore homemade costumes if they were available. We always had masks that seemed scary to us. Our fun was calling on older neighbors who pretended to be terrified by us. We'd often end up at one home for hot chocolate and cookies.

Most of our Halloween parties were at our churches, given by Sunday School teachers. We did not dress up for them, but gathered for games and bobbing apples in a large galvanized tub or going after apples hanging on strings in doorways. For the latter, we had to keep our hands behind us and catch the dangling apple in our mouths with only a set number of tries. If victorious, the apple was the prize.

Sometimes friends had parties during this season and we were costumed for that. There was always a fortune-teller, usually an older woman dressed like a gypsy. She would be placed in a dimly lighted room in a large chair. We were called in one at a time to hear our destinies. She pretended to read palms, but usually gave us a lot of complimentary hopefuls for our lives.

I recall once being told I would become a famous movie actress—which was meant to be thrilling. However, I said to the palmist, "I hope not because Mama says they are fast women, wear too much make-up, and smoke cigarettes. I don't think I would like that very much."

The seer looked utterly shocked at such a report from an 8-year-old. Looking back I wasn't very tactful. However, she was a good friend of my mother's and called her promptly to report my surprising response. It made for much laughter between the two and I was told about it repeatedly much later.

Our refreshments were usually hot chocolate with whipped cream on top and cookies. All were homemade. As we grew older we had "wiener roasts" and marshmallows to place on the end of our sticks for toasting. I remember setting the candies on fire more often than having them reach a delicate, soft brown, as intended. But we liked them every way.

It was truly a simple way of life and most enjoyable. I cherish the way our parents were always there to help with activities. It's long been my belief that children who grow up in small towns have many advantages, simply because that is what happened to me.

Following are some recipes from *Americus Recipes*, a little cookbook I treasure. I have selected some similar to the ones we were served and recognize the names of the contributors as those who might have given a party for us.

Carrot Cookies

3/4 cup low-fat shortening
1 cup granulated sugar
1 cup cooked, mashed, fresh carrots
2 cups all-purpose flour, unsifted
1/4 teaspoon salt
2 teaspoons baking powder
1/2 teaspoon lemon extract
1/2 teaspoon vanilla extract
Grated rind of one orange
1 egg, beaten
1 cup raisins
Icing:
1 cup confectioners' sugar, unsifted
2 tablespoons vegetable shortening, melted
2 to 3 tablespoons fresh orange juice
1 tablespoon grated orange rind

Cream shortening and sugar. Add remaining ingredients in order listed. If raisins are slightly warmed in an oven they combine more easily with the batter. Drop by teaspoonful on ungreased cookie sheet or sheets. Bake one sheet at a time on center rack at 375 degrees for 15 minutes. Remove. while hot and cool on racks.

Apply icing made as follows: mix together all ingredients. Blend well to obtain easy spreading consistency. More orange juice may be needed if too stiff. Yields 3 1/2 to 4 1/2 dozen frosted cookies. Store in tins with waxed paper in between layers to avoid frosting sticking to other cookies. Freeze well. Recipe can easily be doubled. Note: Frosting may be omitted if avoiding sugar.

Brown Sugar Cookies

2 egg whites
1 cup dark brown sugar
3 tablespoons flour
2 cups pecans, chopped fine

Beat egg whites until stiff. Fold in sugar then flour. Add nuts. Drop from spoon on greased baking sheets. Bake about 10 minutes at 350 degrees. Makes about 30 cookies, depending upon amount of mixture used in each spoon. Store in air tight tins when cool.

Pull Candy Parties

How many of you have ever enjoyed a "candy pull" party? They're lots of fun. The pulling is entertaining and the finished product provides refreshments.

I associate candy pulls with the cane-syrup season in southwest Georgia. Every farmer, like my father, always planted a patch of sugar cane for family enjoyment. Much of it was saved for grinding and making into syrup.

Few farms in the area where I grew up were without individual grinders. They were hitched to a mule who pulled the equipment in a circle. The weights attached to the grinder crushed the cane. It was either made into the syrup at home or taken somewhere to be processed. Ours was always driven over in large containers to the little town of Huntington. There was equipment in the town for making large batches of the sweet product. You have probably seen similar mule rigs at places like Jarrell's Plantation, Westville, or other reconstructed farms or villages of the past.

The poor mule walked for hours in circles grinding the cane. He was often changed in rotation to go in the opposite direction to keep him from falling over in dizziness. Usually he had a blinder on one eye to keep the animal from realizing that his circular motion never varied. I don't exactly remember. I always felt sad for the beast, but I certainly enjoyed the results of his work.

When we would make our trips to nearby Huntington, my daddy held me up to look into the huge vats to see the boiling juice. It would cook in this manner for several hours before being thick enough to become syrup. Once it was completed, it was put in covered gallon buckets and brought home. I can still see the rows of those precious cans on our pantry shelf. They were shared with family and friends who didn't have farms, but we always had a quantity on hand.

We were always offered tastes of the fresh cane juice, but I preferred chewing my own cane and extracting the sweet liquid myself. I'm sure Daddy must have worn out several sharp knives peeling and cutting the cane into wedges for Lelia and me, and for our neighborhood friends. He was ever so patient with all of us. We were overjoyed when he would hit a joint in the stalk and leave a little of the juicy part on it along with a strong sliver of the peel. We pretended these were pipes by holding the end of the peeling in our mouths. The circular joint was, in our minds, very similar to a smoking pipe bowl.

There were so many great recipes made with this delicious syrup, which brings me back to the beginning of this story. The syrup candy was always a delight and was often used as a party theme. The recipe for it is given today and may prove of pleasure to some of you and your children.

For a party of this kind, we would assemble and the mother in the household would be making the candy. When it was ready to be pulled, we would grease our hands with butter, choose a partner, then take a glob of the sticky candy into our hands. Naturally it had to be slightly cooled for handling.

Once we received the mass, each of the two partners would take hold of the candy, stand about three feet apart while holding our portion and pulling against each other. We would then walk back to our partner's hands, put our candy together, divide it again and return back the desired amount of candy, pulling the mass as we walked. This was repeated until the rope was about 1 1/2 to 2 inches in width. The faster we worked the more quickly we reached our goal. Once it became a light color and barely sticky, it was either put on a marble slab for cutting or onto greased cookie sheets. Our moms would cut it into about two-inch pieces for us to enjoy when it became thoroughly dry. Our procedure was continued until all of the batch had been completed. Hands were washed, and we would eat hardily.

There was always much laughter accompanied with the pulling. Each couple would vow that they had done the best job and competition for completing the first lot was strong. We thought it was lots of fun and certainly an easy and enjoyable way to entertain young people.

The recipe follows along with several others from my paternal Hooks family. I can't end a column on cane syrup without saying that always my sister and I looked forward to the breakfasts that featured this sweet. It was not only put on waffles, pancakes, and French toast, but Daddy would poke a big hole in the center of a large biscuit, using his thumb and leaving the bottom secure. He would then fill the center with this delicious treat, hand it to us and wait to see the big smiles that followed once we bit into it.

Pulled Syrup Candy

1/2 gallon cane syrup
4 tablespoons butter
1 pound sugar
1 teaspoon lemon extract, if desired
Rind of 1 lemon
Juice of 2 lemons

Mix syrup, butter and sugar. Bring to a boil and add lemon extract and rind. Stir occasionally. Boil for about 3 hours or until a spoonful, if dropped on a plate, will be found stiff enough to be manageable. Add lemon juice just a few minutes before candy is removed from heat. Pour at once onto marble slab or buttered plates. Pull immediately with well-buttered hands. When getting too hard to pull and beginning to dry, place string of candy on buttered surface. Cut into desired size pieces. This makes a large amount and was typical for a "Pulling Party" but can easily be halved or quartered for family use.

Syrup Pudding

2 cups cane syrup
1 cup hot water
3/4 cup vegetable shortening, lard, margarine or butter, room temperature
4 1/2 cups flour
2 teaspoons soda
1 teaspoon baking powder
1/2 teaspoon salt
1 teaspoon nutmeg

Put syrup, hot water and shortening into a bowl. Mix well. Add flour, soda, baking powder, salt and nutmeg together. Sift into the liquid, mix until smooth and pour into a greased pan. Bake at 350 degrees for 30 to 40 minutes or until soft but lightly brown on top. Serve warm with whipped cream or your choice of hot sauces. Makes 8 servings.

During my growing up days, boxes were very important to all of us. Most of the children had great uses for them and so did our parents. The girls liked shoe boxes to make doll or paper doll furniture. The boys liked them for keeping extra marbles, carpentry items, and other collections.

When making doll furniture, we'd take the top off the shoe box. We positioned the lid perpendicular to the box, making the lid appear as a headboard. This made a super small doll bed. Naturally, we'd have to fill the center with cushions or cloth of some sort.

Tables were easy to envision by turning the box part upside down. We sometimes made couches by placing the box lengthwise with the top inserted for a back rest. They looked very real to us. Every time we purchased new shoes we anticipated how we might use our containers.

Mama kept lots of little odds and ends in her boxes, and Daddy used several for fishing tackle. Leila and I each had one for our collections of Indian spearheads. Every time a new field was plowed on our father's farm many of these choice relics would be turned up to the surface. He usually brought them to us, but on occasions we found some for ourselves. I can't imagine whatever became of ours. I would love to have them right this minute for my grandchildren.

Cigar boxes were extremely choice. I don't know just how we came to have them since nobody in my immediate family smoked cigars. But surely friends or family members shared. They were sturdy, little wooden containers with attached tops.

But I must get back to shoe boxes because they were a real treat at least once a year in our Harrold Avenue neighborhood. The boxes served as the raw material for a parade of "street cars" that the children would pull down the sidewalk.

It took almost a full day to prepare our individual cars. Windows would be drawn around the outside of the box and then had to be cut out. That was hard for our small hands and usually required adult help. We

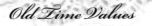

sometimes drew around cookie cutters to make our windows different.

Once the cardboard had been cut out for the window we spent much time pasting colored paper over it. This had to be attached on the inside of the box which made it very clumsy. But it never showed from the outer surface so smears of flour-and-water paste were not noticed on the exterior.

Once this was completed the top had to be cut with a wide opening since a candle stub would go beneath it. By having enough open surface, the object was less likely to catch on fire. Naturally it remained uncovered.

Now we needed to attach a string to the front for ease in pulling our car along behind us. When the appointed time arrived, we would congregate at one house. Then we lined up and walked like a little parade of lighted, colored boxes.

I can see Mama now dripping melted wax into the bottom of our boxes and then sticking the candle piece firmly onto it. She would always light it first to be sure that the above opening was proper. It had to be wide enough for the flame to be completely free from the edges.

At the appointed hour, our group would start at one end of our long block and pull these lighted cars along behind us. Parents were always close by in case a candle might overturn and set our treasure on fire. That happened occasionally with some of the rough boys.

Those of us who tried to make artistic "street cars" looked down on friends who just cut plain holes or squares in their boxes. They didn't even try to cover them colorfully. But everybody was invited to participate if they desired.

As soon as our candles burned low, they were replaced by new stubs until our parade ended. Most of us had the same curfew so we concluded our activity at the same time. We'd also run out of tiny candle bits after a while. Generally one parent on our street was host and served cookies to us.

It seems amazing now that these once treasured boxes are tossed so freely. They were certainly treated with great respect during my youth. Following are recipes typical of what host families served or prepared.

Jam Cake

1 cup butter
1 cup sugar
5 eggs
3 1/2 cups flour, sifted
1 teaspoon cinnamon
1 teaspon allspice
1 teaspoon ground cloves
3 1/2 teaspoons baking powder
1 cup milk
1 cup seeded jam of your choice

Cream butter and sugar. Add eggs one at a time, beating constantly. Sift flour with spices and baking powder and add to first mixture along with milk and jam. Blend well. Bake in 2 layers at 325 degrees for approximately 30 minutes. Frost with white frosting or cream cheese icing. Note: Blackberry jelly may be used in place of jam. This is a good way to use up any jams that might have sugared.

Corn Pudding

1 pint grated corn or equivalent in canned cream corn
1 tablespoon flour
1 teaspoon salt
2 egg yolks beaten
2 tablespoons melted butter
2 egg whites beaten stiff
1/2 cup milk
Pepper to taste

Mix all ingredients together except egg whites. Blend well. Fold in egg whites and pour into a buttered casserole. Bake at 350 degrees for 20 minutes or until pudding tests done when blade of knife inserted comes out clean. Serve hot to 6.

I recently was on a trip to my hometown of Americus. A group of us went by bus for a visit as one of the Back Road Tours sponsored by Macon Heritage Foundation. It brought back many fond memories for me and seemed to be enjoyed by the others who joined us.

When our vehicle passed the little white brick Furlow Grammar School, I all but jumped off the bus to attend classes. I attended there for seven years. It was never referred to as an elementary place of learning, but always as printed above. We had no middle or junior high schools but went directly to Americus High from this first place of learning.

I could almost instantly visualize our precious principal, the late Miss Sarah P. Cobb, standing on the top of the front steps ringing a big bell which called us in for classes. We lined up in front and marched to strains of piano music into our class rooms.

Thinking back on Miss Sarah, she was a unique and warm person. I was sure that she must have been at least 100 years old when I attended. However I have researched her family to find that she was the oldest and not even 60 when I was a student.

A petite woman, she wore her gray hair pulled back in a tight little bun. Her skirts were always long and her clothes very plain. She came from a well-endowed and prominent family, but her dress was the stereotype anyone would have expected her to choose. She did many remarkable things for "her children" during the long years that she taught and served as principal.

She was so distressed by the many youngsters attending classes there who were very underprivileged that she started a soup kitchen. This was done in order to be assured that they had at least one hot meal a day. As far as I know, she was credited with the first attempt at a lunchroom in the state of Georgia.

I can remember going into the building and smelling that delicious soup as it was cooking. It was served in tin cups with a slice of white bread and sold for only a nickel. Imagine! The soup was mostly tomato based with lots of potatoes and onions, and sometimes included a few little canned, green peas. My sister, Leila, and I and many of our friends, were allowed to buy it during winter months or on rainy days. We were delighted to have this warming treat that was provided indoors at recess time. It was served in the basement of the school at long tables.

The children who could not pay for the soup were never noticed by any of us. Our principal was careful not to hurt feelings. I remember seeing some of the group pulling their bread into strips and dunking it into the hot broth. That was new to me, but, of course, I tried it and thought it was delicious.

Miss Sarah was also interested in the health of her group. Once a month we were lined up and taken by classes to be weighed and measured in her little office. A report was sent to our parents with helpful suggestions if we needed to gain or lose weight or if any unusual health problem might be noticed.

This same dear woman had taught my parents during her early years as an instructor. My parents married at early ages, so the span of years for Miss Cobb had not been as great as it may seem from teaching them and then being principal for their children.

Her father, John A. Cobb, has been credited with naming the town Americus (masculine for Amerigo, the first name of the Italian settler of our country, Vespuccio). The Western continents bear his name as the Americas, but not the same as my little home town is credited with having. I researched this information at the Washington Memorial Library in Macon.

Cobb, a large land owner, had moved from Lee County to the newer Sumter. The city was founded in 1832 and given its present title. It is apparently the only town in our country bearing the name of this outstanding explorer.

The Cobb family entertained constantly and naturally produced many excellent cooks. I was delighted to find one, in my Americus cookbook, by my precious Miss Sarah. Two family ones are included here.

Miss Mattie Cobb's Old-fashioned Doughnuts

1 1/2 pints flour
1 cup sugar
1 1/2 heaping teaspoons baking powder
1/2 cup sweet milk
1 teaspoon vanilla
1 tablespoon melted butter
1 egg white, beaten
Powdered sugar for coating
Deep fat for frying

Mix flour, baking powder and sugar, together. Add milk, vanilla and melted butter, mixing well. Finally add beaten egg white. Roll out and cut with doughnut cutter. Fry in smoking hot vegetable shortening. Drain on paper towels and coat with powdered sugar.

Miss Sarah's Coconut Filling

3 tablespoons flour
2 cups sugar
1 cup sweet millk
4 tablespoons butter
1/2 teaspoon vanilla flavoring
2 cups grated, fresh coconut

Mix flour and sugar. Add milk and butter. Boil vigorously for 3 minutes, stirring all the time. Cool and add vanilla and coconut. Spread on cake at once.

Pecan Season

The Lord is so good to provide us with rich Georgia pecans prior to the holiday season. According to the Georgia Agricultural Statistics Service in Athens more than 100 million pounds are often gathered in our state. These nuts begin coming into our markets in early October, but are more bountiful later and seem larger in size. They can be purchased shelled or in the shells, but I am lazy and prefer the former.

Growing up we had pecan trees in our backyard and there were also many on my father's farms. I can remember his bringing them into town in large croker sacks. The early ones were often still in their green shell covering. They needed to be dried out and were poured over paper lined floors on the sleeping porch of our house. This area was usually vacated for warmer parts of the house by mid-September and would be quite vacant by Fall.

The afternoon sun shone brightly on the carefully spread out nuts for several weeks. Eventually the green coverings would turn brown, open at the ends and display the pecan inside. This was the time to hull and shell them for family use. Many times the outer hulls would drop off without our pulling them apart.

Leila and I earned our Christmas shopping money by "picking out" the nut meats from their shells. They would be cracked for us, or we would use hand crackers ourselves on the hard shells to release bits. We were given nut picks to pull out the tiny meats. We tried very hard to get out complete halves, but it was sometimes impossible.

Mother had jars or bowls set out for the whole pieces and also for the tiny ones. She used some recipes with just the halves and others with the smaller pieces. All were valuable to the Thanksgiving and Christmas cooking in our home.

We would sit on the floor by an open fire with newspapers spread beneath us to catch stray shells. Our work was steady. It was a fun conversational time with just the three of us talking about events of the day or plans for the holidays. We were usually paid on Friday nights in order to have our money ready for Christmas shopping or other needs on Saturday when school was out.

Once we had finished shelling for the day, it was fun to watch Mother pour the empty shells onto the fire. It would blaze brightly and offer intense heat.

My friend Nathalie DuPree, of cooking fame, promotes the idea of using pecan shells over outdoor cooking fires. She believes that the shells offer a special flavor to meats being prepared. We were not aware of this in the days of which I am writing, but I honestly don't recall cook-outs when I was a child.

I vividly remember one pecan extraction day when Leila caught me pretending to pull out small nut meats, but I was really cheating. My fingers had grown sore and I simply felt I needed a break. What a pity I didn't confess, for Mother was most understanding. Naturally I was not only reprimanded for my misdeed, but my fee at the end of the week was not as great as my sister's. It was fair treatment but on payday I regretted my dishonesty.

This was not a daily experience, but we spent many hours at this work. Getting paid for doing the work was rewarding, but also the thoughts of all the goodies Mother made using pecans was a real delight.

Most families in our area had their own trees. If not, sharing the unshelled pecans was a way of life. In small communities, like we had, it was considered a delight to help out the neighbors or family members who were not as lucky as we. Consequently they in turn shared any bounty of their homes if others were lacking. It was a pleasant way of life.

My sister and I were usually given some of Mother's baked goods for our Christmas gifts to teachers at school and church. They were always gratefully accepted and we were proud to have played a part in preparing some of the ingredients.

Mother had so many good recipes with pecans that today I shall not ramble on in my past for such length, but instead I will give you some of her tested recipes along with those of her close friends and relatives. Her nut cake was particularly popular. It was often made as gifts for new neighbors or shut-ins as well as for family use. She always gave one to her mother on Mother's Day by request.

Mama's Nut Cake

1 1/2 pounds raisins
1 pound flour
1/2 pound butter
1 pound sugar
6 eggs
1 teaspoon baking powder
1 nutmeg, grated, or 1 teaspoon nutmeg powder
1 cup milk
1 quart pecan halves

Cut raisins and flour them with some of measured amount. Cream butter and sugar. Add eggs, one at a time,. Mix in flour, baking powder and nutmeg alternately with milk. Finally fold in raisins and pecans. Bake at 350 degrees for 1 hour and 15 minutes to 1 1/2 hours or until center of cake tests done. This makes a very large cake and stores well in tight cake container.

Caramel Pecan Candy

1/2 cup cream
1/2 cup cold water
1 tablespoon white corn syrup
Large pinch of salt
1 pound light brown sugar
1 cup chopped pecans

Add cream, water, syrup, and salt to sugar. Cook for 3 to 4 minutes. When candy makes a soft ball, if a small amount is dropped into cold water, remove from heat. Beat well, add pecans and mix thoroughly. Pour into buttered platter. Cut into serving pieces when cool.

Thanksgiving With Family

Thanksgiving. What a wonderful family day it has been for most of us over the years. It bothers me that Christmas decorations are everywhere in our local stores with no signs of this wonderful holiday which occurs first. How thankful we should feel for so many fine advantages in our country while others are war-torn and hunger is ravaging.

When I look back it is with great pleasure. I was certainly one fortunate child with loving parents, grandparents and even very close aunts and uncles. All of them were so good to me and many of us gathered for Thanksgiving dinner at the home of grandparents. Most of us lived in the same small town and those who didn't would come back sometimes during the holiday season.

As a very young child I recall that we had a most unusual treat for our feast. Daddy was a great hunter and well known for his turkey expertise. He could call them up with a little wooden box that scraped over chalk-coated sides. He could make it sound just like a gobbler. Consequently he generally presented the family with a big, wild bird for this feast day. And boy, did Mama ever know how to cook it to perfection. As hunting laws became more restricted, this early childhood delight had to be canceled.

In late August, one year, Daddy brought in a small turkey hen that was put in a cage in our back yard. My sister, Leila, and I, immediately named her Sally and were delighted with our new pet. During the day she was let out of her cage in our fenced back yard and would follow us around like a puppy. She was a most unusual pet and we adored her.

I distinctly remember the evening meal we were having about three weeks prior to Thanksgiving. Daddy asked Mother if she thought Sally was plump enough for the big meal that was forthcoming. Knives and forks dropped and Leila and I shrieked. "You're not killing our Sally to be eaten. We can't stand the thought." It had never occurred to either of us that the new pet had come to our home to be served for dinner. We cried huge tears and begged for the life of our darling pet.

Being the tender parents they were, we were immediately assured that another bird would be purchased. Mama consoled Daddy about the extra expense of a second fowl by remarking that Sally was laying such grand, rich eggs that she had more than paid for herself. "I'll have plenty of these grand eggs to use for my own holiday baking and can share some with relatives and neighbors," she added.

So the life of Sally was extended. The next summer she got out of her cage one night and was killed by some roaming animal that had managed to get into our yard. But we were released from being "cannibals" on that particular Thanksgiving day with our precious pet.

We usually ate our meal at our maternal grandparents' home, Leila Crisp and Fred Davenport. Mother would cook the turkey, oysters, sweet potato casserole, ambrosia and pecan cake. Grandmother prepared a fresh pork roast, the dressing, cranberry jelly, rice and pork gravy, hot biscuits and appropriate vegetables. Mother's only sister, Mary Ella, her husband, Quimby Melton, and their two, much younger sons, Quimby Jr. and Fred, almost always joined us for this day. They lived in Griffin and it was always a treat to have them come for any visit, but especially on this day.

All of the children usually sat at the "kiddie" table and were served first by our parents. As we progressed in age we moved up to the "big" table. But we were always in the same room with the rest of our family. It was truly a warm, happy occasion.

Now for some of the good recipes that we enjoyed.

Cranberry Sauce

1 quart ripe cranberries
1/2 cup water
1 pound sugar

Wash berries well. Place in large saucepan with water. Stew over low heat slowly and frequently particularly after they burst. Add sugar, continue stirring and stewing. Mixture should be like a marmalade when done. Pour into desired mold or dish for chilling and serving. Will become more firm when cold. If desired, press hot mixture through sieve if jellied sauce is preferred.

Mama's Scalloped Oysters

1 quart oysters
Saltine crackers, crumbled enough to use for layering
1/2 cup butter
Salt and pepper to taste
1 cup milk
1 teaspoon Worcestershie sauce

Pick over oysters and remove any shells. Make a layer of oysters with some juice in bottom of baking dish. Layer over with cracker crumbs, enough to absorb some of the liquid. Dot with butter. Continue layering until all oysters and crackers are used. Mix milk and Worcestershire. Pour over all. Top with crumbs. More butter may be added in dots on top of casserole. Bake 30 minutes at 325 degrees. Serves 8 to 10.

Southern Sweet Potato Pie

1 1/2 cups cooked sweet potatoes
1/2 cup brown sugar
1/4 cup granulated sugar
1 teaspoon each ground ginger and cinnamon
1/2 teaspoon salt
1/2 stick butter, melted
1 1/2 cups scalded milk
2 eggs, well beaten
1 (9-inch) deep pie shell
Pecan halves for topping, optional

Beat ingredients together. Pour into unbaked pie shell. Decorate top with pecan halves, if desired. Bake for 20 minutes in preheated 350 degree oven. If edges of pie crust are not brown bake an additional few minutes. Serve hot or cold to 8.

How in the world did I ever get this far into the Fall months without telling you about dishes we enjoyed with sweet potatoes? They were always a part of our Thanksgiving and Christmas dinners either candied or in the casseroles that I've given today. We usually had the latter for turkey day, and they were most often candied for Christmas.

We liked them both ways, and I believe that my maternal grandmother, Leila Crisp Davenport, had the best candied ones ever. I've tried and tried to duplicate them, but they have never tasted as good. Perhaps cooking on the wood stove made a difference. Hers were truly like pieces of candy. The family children liked to take off the sugared top slices and dip up the surrounding syrup to pour over them. What a treat! Mother's were good too, but never were anybody's as special as Grandmother's. The whole family felt this way about them, not just the children.

We enjoyed sweet potatoes for many meals. They are so full of vitamins and other good nutrients that eating them often is not just a delight, but also nutritious. Leila and I were particularly pleased to have them at breakfast. These would be the fried ones, served hot with country butter and crisp bacon on the side.

Sometimes Mother had left-over baked potatoes and would fry them in the same manner as the raw ones, but it would take less time. They were good too, but had to be eaten with a fork. I recall these with breakfasts and some suppers the same as the above. I never remember having either at other meals, but perhaps we did. You may think that it was strange for us to have sweet potatoes for breakfast, but it was common practice in our part of the world. And they were always a great treat to start our day.

Our cook came early enough to prepare breakfast before we left for school. This freed Mother to help us get dressed, hair fixed, teeth brushed, and our tin lunch boxes packed. If there was leftover homework, we had parents free to help us with that too.

My father had grown up on the family plantation and brought many of these delicious food ideas into our family. There's a darling story about him as a little boy in connection with sweet potatoes. His father, the late Thomas Barden Hooks, had built a small, one-room school house for his three boys, their nearby cousins and all of the black children on the farm to attend. My grandfather wanted all the children on his place to know how to read and write. The black children attended his school with the others, which seemed normal to all of them since they played together daily after classes. Could this have been one of the first integrated schools in the state? I've often wondered.

A teacher was hired to instruct the children. She boarded with my father's family. She is the one who passed the following story on about Daddy and the potatoes. It was one day when the word sweet potato had been in their daily work. My father, to her amazement, had spelled the first part of the word correctly but he ended it with "tater." She called him quietly to her desk to set him straight.

"Glenn," she said, "as many good potatoes as your father grows on this farm, how could you spell the word as you did? It is PO-tato and I want you to remember that and learn to correct it next time. Remember that it is PO-tato and not 'tater.'"

"But Miss Annie," he responded in amazement, "My daddy grows GOOD 'taters,' not PO ones."

Now for a few recipes. The candied one is NOT my grandmother's, but then it is as close as I felt I could get to it. I researched in several Southern cookbooks for this and feel that it is adequate. The other was in the family.

Candied Sweet Potatoes

4 medium to large size sweet potatoes
1 cup sugar or more, depending on sweetness desired
4 to 6 tablespoons butter
1/2 cup boiling water

Boil potatoes until half done, peel and slice lengthwise, about 1/3-inch thick. Into a buttered baking dish put a layer of potatoes, dot with butter and sprinkle with sugar until all is used. Pour in water around edges of dish. Top with sugar and butter. Bake at 300 degrees until done and syrup around potatoes is thick. Bake for about 40 minutes. Tops of potatoes should still be sugar coated and juice around them should be a thick syrup. Serve hot.

Fried Sweet Potatoes

Desired number of sweet potatoes
Cooking oil, bacon drippings or butter

Scrub and wash potatoes well. Peel and cut slices lengthwise in 1/4 - inch slices. Fry in butter or cooking oil until soft when pricked with a fork. Use just enough grease to make potatoes brown and turn easily in pan. Drain on paper towels. Serve hot with fresh butter.

Leila and I always anticipated Saturday nights when we were growing up. It was not a school night, so lessons didn't have to be prepared. Consequently, other delights developed. Daddy usually came home a little earlier and always carried *The Saturday Evening Post* under his arm. This nickel magazine was a favorite with us Hookses.

My sister and I would climb into his lap and discuss the Norman Rockwell cover of that week's issue, a delightful part of every publication. We scarcely allowed our father to see the table of contents before we would clamor to view the new Campbell's Soup kids in each edition. Leila and I would cut out these darling prints for paper dolls.

Mama generally prepared a light supper. My sister and I set the table, allowing our father time to read *The Americus Times Recorder*, our afternoon paper. We always subscribed to *The Macon Telegraph* for the morning news.

After our meal, we often played simple card games or Parcheesi, our favorite board game. The games were halted when it was bath time.

Normally we bathed ourselves, but for Sunday events Mama gave us a thorough cleaning. She would scrub behind our ears and even into them as well as our noses. Emphasis was also put on hands and toes. Following the bath, our nails were cleaned or clipped as needed.

While she worked on us, Daddy polished our shoes. Our summer shoes were white and required polishing. Daddy took a great deal of time with them because nobody wanted to see the white polish rub off on our Sunday clothes. Our winter footwear was easier since we usually had black patent leather slippers that only needed a gloss.

Then we chose dresses for the next day. Underwear and matching socks were placed with each outfit.

Generally there was a bit of time left over and our parents and the two children would gather in front of a big coal fire on cold nights like these. Daddy read us stories. He liked to read nursery rhymes. To his delight, we could soon recite them.

Fairy tales were also popular as were "Little Red Riding Hood" and "Cinderella" along with a few other classics. A Bible story generally ended the session. They were mostly from the Old Testament and were exciting. New Testament stories were featured at church Sunday.

I particularly liked hearing about Moses being floated in a basket on the river as a baby. I could easily picture this in my mind, though our book had nice plates in color.

Joseph and his coat of many colors was another prize, but I believe my all-time favorite was Daniel in the lions' den. I couldn't imagine a young boy so brave. The same was true of David killing Goliath.

If the night was a cold one, and we were to leave the warm, open fire to get into our chilly beds, Leila and I held little fuzzy doll blankets close to the fire until we could feel the warmth. Then we'd bundle them close to our chests, run to our beds and slip the heat around our feet as we slid in between the cold sheets. We'd talk for a little while until we were overheard and told it was time to go to sleep.

On summer Saturday nights, we went on the front porch after supper. There was a big chain-type swing at one end, and all four of us would sit in it. Daddy would tell us Uncle Remus stories to our delight. He knew many that I have never seen in Joel Chandler Harris' book. Believe me, Daddy knew the dialect well and also added much with his own little sound effects. Many times the children in the neighborhood would join us for this treat.

When we grew older our parents believed in our knowing good literature. We progressed from the Tom Sawyer books to many Charles Dickens ones. I also remember *Miss Minerva and William Green Hill* and others popular at the time. Reading has been a joy for me all these years.

Forget the electronics and enjoy a good book. You can't beat it. I learned that a long time ago.

Now here are a couple of our favorite recipes.

Salmon croquettes

1 (3 1/2-ounce) can red salmon
1 medium onion, chopped fine or diced
1 raw egg
4 to 6 buttery type crackers, coarsely crumbled
1/4 teaspoon baking powder
.Finely chopped parsley
Oil for deep frying
Additional cracker crumbs

Debone and mash salmon well. Add next 5 ingredients mixing well. Roll and shape into oblongs, about 2 inches in diameter. Roll each in additional cracker crumbs. Fry in hot oil until golden brown. Drain on paper towels and serve hot to 4. (These can be baked for about 30 minutes, or until frim and lightly brown, at 350 degrees if you are not allowed fried foods. Mother always fried hers. I have made smaller ones of these and served them as appetizers. They are good cold, but best hot.)

Southern Biscuits

2 1/2 cups flour
3 teaspoons baking powder
1 teaspoon salt
1/2 cup lard or shortening
3/4 cup milk

Heat oven to 450 degrees. Mix dry ingredients and cut in shortening until mixture resembles peas. Stir in milk mixing well. Round up dough on a lightly floured board. Knead very lightly. Roll out to about 1/2-inch thickness. Cut in rounds and place on ungreased cookie sheets. Bake for 10 to 12 minutes. Makes about 20 biscuits, 3-inches in diameter size or fewer large ones.

Buttermilk may be substituted for regular milk if desired. If so, reduce baking powder to only 2 teaspoons and add 1/2 teaspoon baking soda and 2 more tablespoons shortening. This bread should always be served very hot with plenty of fresh butter.

Jumping Rope

I was interested in a front page story recently about how popular jump rope is becoming. Quite frankly I don't know how the children in Americus would have survived without this great sport when I was a child. As young girls, we had individual ropes with handles on their ends to jump solo. Or we could call in a partner to jump with us, if one was present. But mostly they were ever available at our homes to enjoy outdoors alone. My sister Leila, my friend, Martha Marshall, and I, were allowed to use them on our front porches on rainy days.

The individual ropes were also carried to school to be used during recess time. However, we often used large and long ropes there in order for many children to jump at the same time. There would be two throwers or holders of the ends of this long, heavy cord and the players would line up to take turns. The handlers were changed periodically in order for all to join the fun. I remember one girl who preferred to throw and not jump. She was naturally quite constantly in demand.

I recall that when a jumper would watch the rope swing her way for a long time we'd grow impatient. If she hesitated for any continued period of time before running into the swinging rope to jump we'd all say, "Stop eating gnats and run in and jump." I can't imagine where we got that saying, but it always worked.

It was difficult to time the swing of the rope and new players were cautious. If you straddled the hemp then you were out and lost a turn. That was easily done as one would run into the game. And of course, if you ever stepped on the cord during any jump you were immediately out, and the next player proceeded into the game.

Sometimes we did not swing the rope overhead but rocked it, first slowly and then quite hard. The object for the jumper was to be quick and fast and avoid straddling the rope. This way was called "rocking the cradle." The method of swinging would usually be decided by the entire group and also the fast or slow games.

"Salt, pepper, vinegar, mustard hot peas!" called for swift throwing and quick jumping. We were all quite good at this sport and I can see how the exercise was beneficial. I wish that I could indulge in this action today, but it exhausts me even to think about it.

All of our jumping was done to little rhymes or sayings that we had. I recall a number. Some of my favorites were: "Ice cream soda with a cherry on the top, tell me the name of your sweetheart." After repeating this with a jump for each word we would then go down the alphabet and if you missed on a certain letter, that determined the initial of our sweetheart or possibly the person we might eventually marry. This was serious business with us and we were ready to tease if a player deliberately stopped on a chosen letter.

A silly one, played in the same manner, was "Last night and the night before, a lemon and a pickle came a'knocking at my door. Went to the door to let them in, knocked me in the head with a rolling pin. As they left I heard them say, a-b-c-d" etc.

Another fun one, I feel certain, was also played with a bouncing ball. The following motions would have to be accomplished as we jumped or as the ball bounced without missing, of course. The saying was, "Teddy bear, teddy bear, turn all around. Teddy bear, teddy bear, touch the ground. Teddy bear, teddy bear, show your shoe. Teddy bear, teddy bear that will do." The object was to complete the entire verse without missing a jump or a bounce of the ball.

I usually wore out my individual rope in a season, and a new one was under my stocking each Christmas. I remember receiving a long rope one year and I found out later that it had to be purchased from a hardware store. That one accompanied me to school many days and I could invite friends to my own game. What simple pleasures these were, but much was to be learned by sharing and complimenting others in the game who were good at the sport. It was just basic good sportsmanship, in my opinion.

My maternal Grandmother Davenport called it "skip rope" and never failed to tell me how good she had been as a child. I felt greatly flattered one day when she said that she thought I had surpassed her old talent. I certainly got enough practice.

She told me about one day when she had gone to her friend Mattie Eldridge's house to "skip rope" with her. The friend's mother told her daughter that she was very sorry, but she could not play until she darned the socks she had been told to repair.

Both girls were distressed over this news, but Mattie said, "Come on, I know how to do this fast." To the astonishment and delight of my grandmother, the child threw her socks on the floor and exclaimed, "Darn it, darn it, darn it" as she quickly jumped over the footwear.

Both girls burst into giggles and went outside to enjoy their fun. Mattie said she could fix those socks that night and her mother would never know the difference. I always thought that was a delightful little story and it certainly appealed to Grandmother for her to have remembered it over the years. This also shows how long jumping rope has been popular with children.

After so much activity in our young years , I'm sure that we must have been quite ready for a hearty meal at the end of the day. Here are some of the delicious recipes that Mother often prepared for us on those cool nights.

Southern Spoon Bread

2 cups milk
2 cups water
1 cup corn meal
2 tablespoons butter
1 3/4 teaspoons salt
3 eggs, well beaten

Mix the water and meal. Cook in a sauce pan until the consistency of thin mush. Add butter, salt, milk and eggs to the mixture. Bake in oven at 400 degrees for 45 minutes. Serve at once from pan with plenty of butter or gravy. (We usually had Mother's homemade sausage or crisp bacon to accompany this dish.) The meat might also have been broiled ham or quail, the latter depending on my father's hunting luck.

Sally Lunn Bread

2 cups flour
1/2 cup sweet milk
1 egg
Butter the size of an egg or about 3 tablespoons
1 1/2 tablespoons sugar
1 teaspoon baking powder

Mix the ingredients together until smooth and pour into a greased, deep pan. Bake at 350 degrees for about 20 minutes. Ovens vary, and this recipe calls for a moderate oven, so perhaps 375 degrees would be a better choice for cooking. The same meats might well accompany this delight.

Baked Apples

4 medium cooking apples, cored
1 tablespoon sugar per apple or more, depending on tartness of fruit
2 teaspoons butter for each apple
Small amount of water

After coring the apples, but not peeling them, fill the cavities with sugar and top with butter. Place in a buttered, deep pan and pour in enough water to cover the bottom. Bake at 375 degrees, uncovered, until tender but not so that the apples will lose their shapes. It takes about 30 minutes. Baste with pan juices a few times while cooking and also when removed from oven. More water may be added if needed for basting. Serve hot or cold with thick cream. Serves 4. (Many people use brown sugar, cinnamon and raisins in the cavity of the apples, but Mother never did. We liked them this way.)

Winter

When I was growing up, evidences of Christmas were not seen until after Thanksgiving. It still seems appropriate to set aside November for Thanksgiving. It's a wonderful holiday that seems to be greatly pushed back in this day and time. As a matter of fact, there was very little evidence of this national holiday in the stores here this year. Christmas decorations were out before Halloween, another fun day. I don't think I'm alone in resenting the fact that these holidays were overlooked to start Christmas promotion.

Leila and I didn't even start writing letters to Santa until after Thanksgiving. That was when most people I knew began to focus on the most outstanding holiday of our year. We still had a whole month to plan and prepare and get excited about the upcoming event. When we scribbled our carefully worded letters to Santa we never failed to tell him what good girls we had been all year. Naturally we felt that this would increase our chance of receiving the requested gifts.

Once they had been carefully written, we'd go to the fireplace and mail them up the chimney in the smoke of a low blaze. After all, if this great man was coming into our house in this flue, the best post-office for him had to be from from that very same spot. We had to lean way over to see them go up in the rising smoke.

Often we'd get Mama or Daddy to poke them high up for us. Sometimes they would catch on fire if we were unable to reach the height required. This meant that we had the writing to do all over again.

I remember one day when I lost two letters to the flames. Daddy tried to comfort me by saying Santa was so magical he felt certain the miracle man knew what I wanted. He didn't think a third writing was necessary, but I was too nervous not to try my letter a third time. This time he practically threw it up the chimney and declared it was well on its way.

The Americus Times Recorder, our town's afternoon newspaper, was good to the children in the community. They would print our letters on a special page if we wrote to Santa in care of them. I took no chances, but wrote to the gracious gentleman both ways.

Once the stores in Americus started putting out their decorations and trimmings it was fun to visit them. Many new items arrived for our attention. My sister and I would go to the big stores just to look at options. We'd observe things that had not previously been on our Christmas lists. This was both true for giving and receiving.

When my sister was in high school she made close friends with Lena (McMath) Small who is still one of our dearest associates. She lived across town from us and had attended the little East Americus Elementary School instead of Furlow Grammar, where we had always gone. One day, soon after the Christmas items were being displayed in the store, these two friends decided to go and look them over.

Leila told me about many of the great things they had seen and where they could be found. Consequently, I told my close friend, Martha (Marshall) Dykes and we planned a trip the next day to look over the situation.

That was the first year I remember seeing Kewpie dolls. (Their title had to be a play on the word Cupid.) The dolls were about a foot high with rather chubby heads and bodies. They had no real hair, but painted, plaster that resembled the real thing. It was designed to turn over in a small curl on top like a dip of Dairy Queen ice cream. Another distinct feature was a cupid's bow mouth, also painted. The eyes were not made to open and close.

My friend and I dashed home after viewing them. We needed to tell our families about these desirable dolls. They were immediately put on our lists to Mr. Claus.

Naturally, on the big day, we both got a doll. They were not movable and not much fun for playing. However, they were unique in our eyes and we made up games that included them. They were also attractive as decorations on our dressers. They were very sturdy and stood well on their slippered feet.

The one that Santa brought me was dressed in pink, and Martha's was in blue. Since we played together so constantly it was necessary to have them distinctive for each child. I don't know if I have seen any of these treasures that were so popular in our youth. I'm sure doll collectors could tell us more about them, but I've not had a chance to check it out.

$$\infty \sim$$

Flaky Pecan Party Biscuits

2 cups sifted all-purpose flour
3 teaspoons baking powder
3 tablespoons sugar
1/2 teaspoon salt
1/2 cup butter or margarine
1/2 cup pecans, finely cut
1/2 cup milk
1 egg, slightly beaten

Sift dry ingredients together. Cut butter into mixture with pastry blender until it resembles cornmeal. Add nuts. Combine milk and egg and add all at once to dry mixture. Stir well with fork. Turn dough onto a lightly floured board. Knead gently a few times. Roll dough 1/2-inch thick. Cut into 1-inch rounds with floured cutter. Bake on greased cookie sheet at 425 degrees for 12 to 15 minutes. Slit each biscuit and insert butter before serving very hot.

Christmas Ginger Cakes

3 cups flour
1 teaspoon cinnamon
1 teaspoon allspice
1/2 teaspoon ginger
1 teaspoon baking powder
1 teaspoon baking soda
2 eggs
1/4 cup sugar
1/2 cup butter and 1/2 lard, mixed
1/4 cup buttermilk
1/4 cup dark molasses or cane syrup
1 cup broken pecans
1/4 pound raisins

Mix dry ingredients together. Beat eggs until light and blend into first mixture. Add sugar, butter and lard cutting in well. Combine milk and syrup, mixing thoroughly. Add nuts and raisins last, blending well. Batter will be stiff. Drop on greased baking sheets 2 inches apart. Bake at 350 degrees 20 to 30 minutes or until edges and tops are brown. Makes a large quantity.

Christmas shopping for family and friends was one of the fun things of my youth during this season. When real small I would be accompanied by Mama or my older sister, Leila. Family Christmas gifts had to be closely held secrets as did those for my playmates. They were always to be complete surprises for any of the recipients.

We were taught to spend our own money for the various presents. My sister and I made extra shopping cash by picking out pecans for our mother's Christmas baking. If we ran short of funds we could borrow from our parents or each other.

I recall one day, before I was well informed about taking a loan, that I learned a valuable lesson. I must have been six or eight years old when my friend, Martha, and I were looking at gifts for our families. Remember, our town of Americus was small and we were allowed to walk to the stores with older children from our Harrold Avenue homes. This must have been one of those days. We were shopping for family, which meant that Leila was not along.

Martha and I were in our favorite Five and Ten Cent store, the S.H. Kress Co., Kresses we called it. I spotted a bow necktie that I thought would be great for my daddy. By this time I had spent what cash I had on hand and remembered seeing my father on the nearby corner as we passed. I rushed out of the store and found him talking with his brothers, J.D. and Tommy Hooks.

"Let me have a quarter, Daddy, and I will buy you a present that I have just seen and know you will like." This brought hilarious laughter from both of my uncles. It never occurted to me that I was asking him to fork over for his own gift. Of course he gave me the money and I promptly returned to my shopping. I purchased the little black tie with colorful spots. and felt very proud of my good choice

When I returned home I was telling my sister about this. She was horrified. "Why you've asked Daddy to buy his own present from you. That's not really giving," she said. Mama overheard us and agreed that Leila was right. Both offered to promptly lend me the money to pay back my father. I was very ashamed, but glad to have learned a good lesson so gently.

Of course asking Daddy for the quarter to purchase his own Christmas present was the reason for his brothers' instant and hearty laughter at the time. You can understand how embarrassed I felt about all of this later. My father would never have let me know how ridiculous my asking had been. He was strongly opposed to hurting the feelings of anybody, especially those of a child.

Leila and I kept our coins in little banks. Hers was cast iron in the form of a small Statue of Liberty. Being younger, mine was not so elegant but was easier to handle. We often shook the coins out through the slots into which they had been inserted. This was fun and also avoided opening the bottoms of the containers. If the latter was done all of the contents would fall out and possibly spill over the floor. We soon learned that a nail file, poked into the slots, helped us retrive just the amount needed.

One of my most memorable gifts for Martha brought good luck for me as well. Mama and I were shopping together when she spotted some new items being opened at the toy counter in Kresses. They were little doll wash stands, complete with bowl and pitcher.

We both knew that this was a gift of real choice for my constant friend. The little stands were made of wire and metal. They looked sort of like a high chair though much taller. They stood on wire frames with the long legs ending in four curves for balancing. The seat was solid with a hole cut in the center to hold the tub and pitcher. The metal back was also of one piece, probably tin. The surface was encased in the frames.

The solid part was painted blue. The tiny accompaniments were just white and also made of tin. The entire toy was only about ten or twelve inches high. It was perfect for my friend. Mama said that she would tell Martha's mother about my gift is order to avoid duplication. This appropriate present cost a whole quarter, which seemed like a fortune to me. But certainly Martha should be well treated by me at Christmas time.

Mama and I walked home by way of my Grandmother Davenport's to show her our purchases. My grandparents lived across town from us. They were always delighted to see us when we popped in on them.

Grandmother had told Mama that she wanted to enjoy our shopping spree with us. She'd asked for this visit. And what a break it turned out to be for me. She wanted to see the purchases and exclaim with us about our choices.

I could hardly wait to show her the wash stand. She agreed that it was well worth the high price that I had paid. Mama suggested that we cut a tiny piece of soap to resemble a real doll size one. It was made and placed on the side of the bowl. Grandmother suggested making a towel and wash cloth in scale. They could hang across the wire frame at the top of the toy. She promptly produced a blue and white wash cloth and with keen scissors cut both tiny shapes.

This was all so delightful that I was simply elated over such a fun gift. Then came the joy. Grandmother said, "Darling, I've never seen anybody have such a good time with a toy. I think that you should have one too and I'll buy it for you right this minute." She promptly handed me the cost. The next day I returned to my favorite store to purchase my very own. I knew how to complete mine to match that of my friend's. It was also complete with homemade soap and linen.

After Christmas Martha and I probably had the cleanest small size dolls in town. The little stands were too small for big babies, but just right for the others. I can see us now, filing the tiny pitchers, pouring the bath water into the miniature tubs and scrubbing our children well. What wonderful play that afforded us. And wasn't it great of my darling grandmother to treat me before Christmas to such a nice present? No wonder I've never forgotten such a memorable pleasure.

Here I'm offering you some good holiday recipes.

Pecan Ring

1 1/2 cups chopped pecans
1 cup bread crumbs
1 1/2 cups milk
1 cup chopped celery
1/2 cup melted butter
2 eggs, well beaten
2 tablespoons chopped onions
Salt and pepper to taste

Soak bread crumbs in milk and set aside. Saute onion and celery. Mix remaining ingredients together, well, adding eggs last. One fourth cup of chopped nuts should be reserved. Dust the bottom of buttered ring mold with reserved chopped nuts. Pour in mixture and place pan in warm water. Bake at 375 degrees for 45 minutes to an hour or until firm.

Unmold and fill ring with creamed chicken or turkey. A vegetable coated in cream sauce may be substituted for the meat. This is very rich and was only used for special occasions like those of the holiday season. It was always served in homes in my town during this time of the year. When pecans were harvested many hostesses in Americus liked to treat their guests to this delicacy.

Fruit Nut Bars

1 1/2 sticks butter
1 pound dark brown sugar
3 eggs
1 teaspoon vanilla
1 1/2 cups sifted plain flour
2 cups chopped pecans
1 pound mixed crystallized fruit

Line oblong pan with foil, grease and flour. Spread pecans on bottom. Cream butter and sugar. Add eggs, vanilla and flour. Pour over nuts and then spread fruit, that has been dusted with flour over the top. Bake 1 hour at 350 degrees. Allow to cool before removing from pan. Cut in squares. (Note: foil is a new item, since my mother's day, but it is easier to use than just greasing the floured pan.)

Preparing For Christmas

One of our most fun family events before Christmas was going out from Americus to Daddy's farm and gathering the greens for decorating the house. We would usually go on the Sunday afternoon right before the big day unless the holiday fell too close to that Sunday. In that case, we would go two Sundays before Christmas. We wanted to keep the pickings fresh throughout the season, so we never went too early.

Our father was superstitious and felt that all Christmas decorations had to be removed from the house before New Year's Day. If not, bad luck was sure to follow. Consequently, all greens were removed before they became too dry.

It will seem strange to many of you, I'm sure, that we had no Christmas tree until we were older. The early ones were lighted with tiny candles and my parents considered them a fire hazard. This never bothered Leila and me because our entire thoughts of this special holiday centered around Santa Claus. No tree could ever have competed with this jolly old man in our opinions. As we grew older and electric lights were strung on the trees we had one too, but not during our earliest years which were really the most fun.

We were quite happy with the garlands of smilax over the mantles and around pictures. Vases of holly were beautifully arranged by our talented mother and placed in strategic points throughout the living part of the house. There was always mistletoe tied on the living room chandelier with a red velvet ribbon. But the prettiest piece of all was a huge holly wreath, made by Mother, that hung on the entrance door. Of course, it had a big red bow on top that dangled to the bottom curve. I'm still in awe of how she made it so easily.

We would bundle up for these greens-gathering expeditions and drive out in the old Ford to the wooded part of the farm. Daddy would have already spotted holly trees heavy with berries plus the other greens. He took along his shotgun to shoot down the mistletoe. All of us would gather the loot and put it on the floor of the car. I distinctly remember the holly near our legs that would lightly prick us as we bumped along home. Leila and I would draw up our feet onto the back seat of the car in order to avoid extra scratches.

After returning home, while soaking the greens in tubs of water on our back porch, we would clean our hands and get ready for supper.

On such a busy evening Mama would cook a light supper for us. It was often more like breakfast with scrambled eggs, bacon, sausage, and grits. On most winter nights, in fact, our evening meal was a light one. It might be smothered doves with grits, gravy, hot biscuits, and a dessert. Pancakes were also a popular choice and were usually served with fried country ham, country sausage, or bacon. Daddy loved oyster stew, much to my dismay, so it was often served too. The night after gathering the greens, we often enjoyed sampling Christmas cookies.

Mincemeat Drop Cookies

1/2 cup shortening
3/4 cup granulated sugar
1 egg
1 teaspoon vanilla or lemon extract
1 1/2 cups sifted flour, all-purpose
1/2 teaspoon baking powder
1/2 teaspoon salt
3/4 cup mincemeat

Cream shortening and sugar together well. Blend in egg and flavoring, vanilla or lemon. Add flour sifted with baking powder and salt. Mix in mincemeat. Drop by teaspoonful onto greased baking sheets. Bake one sheet at a time in 350 degree oven for about 15 minutes or until lightly brown and slightly dry on edges. Makes about 4 dozen. (These freeze well, but in my Grandmother's day that was unheard of by her generation. We usually ate them up quickly any way.)

Christmas Gems

1 1/2 cups sugar
1 cup soft butter
2 eggs
2 3/4 cups flour
1 teaspoon soda
1/2 teaspoon salt
2 teaspoons cream of tarter
2 teaspoons ground allspice
1 cup raisins
1 cup chopped pecans

Cream sugar, eggs and butter together. Sift flour with baking soda, salt, cream of tarter and allspice. Add to first mixture. Fold in raisins and pecans. Drop by teaspoon on greased cookie sheets. Bake at 375 degrees for 10 minutes or until cookies are brown around edges and lightly tan on tops. Remove from sheets and cool before storing. Makes about 6 dozen.

The beginning of Christmas was marked for our household with a special gift: "Aunt" Mattie Marshall, my close friend Martha's mother, made gorgeous candies.

Aunt Mattie's family always went to Quitman for the big day to be with her mother, the late Mrs. Walter Hunter Sr. Consequently, her large, metal box of assorted candies came to us before December 25.

We expected this treat and it will always seem a part of the holiday treasures. We were allowed to open and enjoy it until the big day. Other gifts had to be saved for tearing into on Christmas Day.

Penuche, Divinity, Taffy, Chocolate Fudge, and, in later years, Martha Washington candies were always included. The Penuche was my favorite. We had fudge and what we called "pull candy" at home. But this light brown sugar confection was one that I shall always associate with Christmas and that dear lady.

Back then it seemed eons from one Christmas to the next. Unfortunately, with age, this holiday appears to arrive almost every few weeks. I can't believe I get through wrapping gifts for one Christmas when before I know it, here comes the next. But I shall always cherish this special day, both past and present.

We heard the beautiful Christmas story at Sunday school each year. It was read and told to us many times before the real day. I don't remember church pageants, but I do recall the First Baptist Church having a seasonal event where the little children sang and recited poems.

My step-grandmother Hooks headed the kindergarten department there for years. She was marvelous with little ones and both my sister and I attended her church during the years we were this age. After she was told about my singing "Happy Birthday to Jesus" on my third Christmas morning she marked me for performing it the next year. I was terrified to stand before the whole congregation and sing, but my parents urged me to do so as did my grandparents. Of course, I did this remarkable feat. But I said I would only stand on the platform and sing if Daddy would sit on the end of a row where I could see him. He declared that he would. He followed my orders and held his head out so far into the aisle I could not miss seeing him. It must have been a horror and most uncomfortable.

Christmas Eve night was so special that I tingle at just the thought of it. After Leila and I hung up our little white knit stockings by the fireplace we went with Mama to the kitchen. There she cut a huge piece of Daddy's birthday cake left over from our celebration of his special day, December 23. It was placed on a saucer for us. Then she poured a glass of homemade scuppernong wine. These were treats for us to leave for Santa.

We always left our snacks on the middle of the mantle piece. This was in the family room where we expected Santa to tumble down the chimney.

Following these traditions we would climb into Daddy's lap and he would read aloud "The Night Before Christmas." Our book was filled with pictures and we'd examine each page carefully. I can still see, in my mind's eye, many of the colored illustrations included.

Next was prayer time. We would kneel against the lap of one of our parents and simultaneously say our "Now I lay me's." This was followed by asking our God to bless practically everybody we could think of, since the longer we prayed, the later we went to bed.

"Good nights" to our parents were now in order along with many kisses, not only to them but to each other as well. Then Leila and I went off to bed in a nearby room.

Excitement was so high by this time that I well remember having difficulty sleeping. I would squeeze my eyes tightly shut. I never remember hearing Mama and Daddy go to bed or seeing that the lights were out. But I recall hearing Santa coming up Harrold Avenue in Americus. I was sure Santa started at the far end of the street because of hearing him and his reindeer at several dwellings.

I distinctly remember one night when he stopped right next door at Brown Small's home. I scurried to the foot of my bed beneath the covers. "You must'nt let Santa find you awake," I'd been told. Hiding snugly this way I fell asleep. Never did I hear his sled on our roof. But I could certainly determine his route of arrival.

Do you know I still listen for him on Christmas Eve? I feel as if he is on his way to me and mine once again. He'd certainly want to join us for some of the delicious candy we had. Recipes follow.

Penuche

2 cups light brown sugar
3/4 cup light cream or rich milk
1/8 teaspoon salt
2 tablespoons butter
1 teaspoon vanilla
1/2 to 1 cup chopped pecans

Combine sugar, cream or milk and salt in a saucepan. Stir constantly over low heat to prevent curdling or sticking. When mixture forms a soft ball, if a small bit is dropped from a spoon into cold water, remove from heat. Add vanilla and butter. Beat hard until mixture becomes creamy. Add nuts and beat to blend well. Drop by teaspoon onto waxed paper or a greased surface. Remove when cool and store. Makes about 1 pound.

Chocolate Fudge

2 cups sugar
2 tablespoons cocoa
1 cup milk
1 teaspoon vanilla
3 tablespoons butter
Pinch of salt
1 cup chopped pecans

Mix sugar and cocoa. Add milk and mix well Cook over moderate heat, stirring often, until a firm ball is formed when a small amount is dropped in cold water. (Candy thermometer will register 236 degrees.) Remove from heat, add butter, salt, and vanilla. Allow to cool slightly then beat well adding pecans last. Beat hard until mixture will stand alone when dropped from a spoon. Drop from spoon on greased surface in desired size pieces. Makes about a pound.

Christmas morning in our home was so exciting that I still get "chilly bumps" just thinking about it.

It was customary for the first person to awaken to yell out, "Christmas gift!" which was a holdover from my father's growing up years on the old family plantation. Whoever managed to say it first was the lucky one. In Daddy's day it meant that everyone who was caught with this exclamation was supposed to give a gift to those who were snared by the alert caller.

Once the words were said, Mother, my sister, Leila, and I had to stay still and warm under our bed covers while Daddy went into the adjoining room where our empty stockings were hung on the previous night. There he would prepare a roaring fire before we were allowed to jump from bed. Remember, these were the days of open fireplaces and not central heat.

The wait for the fire seemed endless. We would call out, "Hurry, hurry with that fire; we can't wait." Quite often, tease that he was, the response would be, "No need to rush. It doesn't look like the old boy brought anything this year. But he's left a note that he ran out of presents and will bring you twice as many next year." Of course, we didn't believe him and didn't have to, because he would either pick up a baby doll and turn it so we could hear the cry or play a note on a doll piano or find some sort of cunning way to reassure us with an enlightening sound.

Once we were robed and slippered we would tear into the room. Leila had one side of the fireplace for her presents and I had the other. Our own little cotton knit stockings that looked so empty when we hung them, would be bulging with goodies. These were not the days of fancy "store-bought" bright red or green stockings. No, they were our very own and extremely stretchable. Grapes and dried raisins on stems were most often pinned to the outside. There were also "dough faces" or funny masks pinned to the toe and most likely a horn sticking out of the top.

We never emptied our stockings immediately since we knew they contained mostly fruits, assorted nuts and those delicious pink, white, green, and yellow bonbons that were coconut filled. We never had them except for Christmas and I was sure that they were made only at the North Pole. A quarter was usually put in the toe of the stocking to entice us to empty them after a few days.

The little white, filled stockings were covered with sooty finger prints that Santa had left after his slide down the chimney. The fireplace would also be covered with soot respective of his jump down the chimney. In addition there would be fingerprints around the cake plate where we had left our precious gentleman large pieces of cake to enjoy while he was treating us.

He sometimes wrote us letters in poetic form and they, too, were smeared with soot. We could not stand to part with anything that the grand old man had touched—which was another reason for allowing our stockings to hang for several days.

Our sought-after gifts were never wrapped, but placed in the area closest to our own stocking. My doll might have been sitting in a tiny high chair or in a carriage, depending on the kind requested. Leila's would be equally prominent in a doll bed or surrounded by new clothes for her baby.

Our other gifts would be real surprises since our parents were clever enough to order through catalogs and find things that we didn't see in stores. Consequently, Santa was so real I never once doubted him even when I was first told. After recalling all of this I'm not sure he isn't real after all.

Right in the middle, between the array of gifts for both girls, would be a selection of fireworks. They were usually stacked in wigwam fashion to be shot that night or later with cousins. Yes, we had them for Christmas and not the New Year. They were as much a part of that celebration as the holly and gifts.

After my sister and I had been given enough time to view all of our treasures and each other's, we would exchange family gifts. We always had something nice from our parents which was another reason for hanging onto Santa for years. We'd most often be holding dolls as we untied our carefully wrapped surprises. It was always grand to hear our parents exclaim with pleasure over our selections for them. They certainly knew how to please us.

After the early morning pleasures of Santa we would be given a light breakfast. We would then put on our clothes and bundle up on journeys to relatives and friends to offer our gifts for them and receive theirs for us.

We would go to our paternal grandparents' first and try to catch them with "Christmas gift!" since this was definitely a part of their day too. We always ate mid-day dinner at our maternal grandparents' home. They lived across town from us and were so delighted with our arrival.

My sister and I would usually take our dolls along with us or some special gifts that we most wanted just for "show and tell." Plus, we wanted some of our Santa Claus to accompany us and not have to stay at home all lonely.

Christmas dinner was very much like Thanksgiving, although not quite as elaborate. There was always turkey and dressing, country ham, biscuits and many of the vegetables used on the earlier holiday.

The big difference was that we had a dessert that Leila and I thought had been made in heaven. We called it Charlotte Russe, but after researching in many cookbooks I find that ours was really White Charlotte, since the other is made with a boiled custard base and lady fingers surrounding it. Also, since daddy's birthday was on Dec. 23, he wanted a coconut cake, and of course mother provided it. We had that with our dessert as well as a chocolate layer cake from grandmother's kitchen. Here is a recipe for that dessert and another associated with Christmas.

Grandmother's Charlotte Russe

2 envelopes (2 tablespoons) plain gelatin
1 cup cold water
1 quart whipping cream, no substitute
1 cup sugar, divided
4 egg whites
3/4 cup sherry
Maraschino cherries for garnishing

Soak gelatin in cold water. Dissolve in a double boiler over hot water. Set aside to cool. Whip cream with 2/3 cup sugar, not too stiff. Slowly add cooled gelatin to the cream and beat thoroughly. Beat egg whites until stiff, but not dry, with remaining sugar. Gently fold into whipped cream mixture and gradually fold in the sherry. Pour into a mold and refrigerate until firm. Unmold on platter and garnish with cherries. This is very rich and could serve 10 to 12.

Turkey Dressing

2 eggs
1/2 cup fine cornmeal
2 cups flour
1 teaspoon baking soda
1 teaspoon salt
1 teaspoon black pepper
2 cups buttermilk
1 onion, chopped
1 cup chopped celery
10 to 12 day old biscuits, or slices of bread, toasted
1/2 stick of butter, melted
Enough stock from fowl to mix into soft batter

Break biscuits or toast into crumbs. Mix in with all other ingredients. Pour into greased, long baking dish or pan and bake for 35 to 45 minutes at 350 degrees. Dressing should be brown on top and leaving sides of pan when done. Cut into squares for serving to a large crowd of about 16 to 20.

Our daddy, Glenn Hooks, grew up on the family farm or plantation, as he preferred to call it. This was about five or six miles from the city of Americus. The place was known as Woodfin.

It included a large house along with many barns, cabins for the helpers and other structures. Cotton fields lay in abundance around the "big" house and its environ.

The family dearly loved the black people on "the place" and played with the children. Daddy and his brothers, Tommy and J.D., often visited them in their houses where they learned many superstitions and stories. Scores of these had been brought from Africa by their forebears. Perhaps some were just made up for their own pleasure. However, they seem interesting to me and I hope you enjoy reading about them too. Our father firmly believed in some of them and passed a number on to his family. My sister Leila and I swore by them as firmly as Daddy. After all, we trusted him completely. I well remember seeing him tip his hat when he saw a rabbit running close to our path or even just in a field. This was sure to bring good luck.

He would get out of the car in which we were riding if a cat of any color crossed our path. Then he would make a cross mark with his foot and spit right in the center of it. Certainly this would dissuade any bad luck. I'm told that many Southerners wearing hats will take them off, turn them around and spit right in the center of the crown to avoid cat troubles. Or maybe some will just turn their hats completely around on their heads.

There were several superstitions that we learned concerning New Year's Day. Christmas decorations must be taken out of the house or off the grounds prior to the new year. If not, you might have bad luck the next twelve months. I still make a point to have mine all down and even put away before the clock strikes twelve on the eve of this holiday. No point in taking chances and I find it easier to pack them away early and get back to normal. On New Year's Day never sweep out the trash or dirt from a house. And clothes should not be washed either. One will mean clearing the house of the dead, and the other washing away luck.

Most of us in the South imagine that hog jowl and peas, cooked and served on this holiday, will bring peace and prosperity to families who enjoy such a tradition. Later years have brought greens (mostly collards) to the table to represent the abundance of money that will come to any who eat them. Naturally, the more consumed of either dish, the wealthier and happier a person will be. But the peas and jowl are an older custom.

Watch the first twelve days of the new year. Any weather that forms will be indicative of what we might expect for the year. The first day will represent January, the second February and so on down the line. Whatever you do on the first day of the year you will find yourself busy with the same throughout the next one. For example, if you are working, then thank goodness your job is secure for another twelve months! If you are entertaining, expect many parties to come your way. Be sure to watch what comes into your life on that first day. It will surely be with you throughout the weeks that lie ahead.

Never point at the stars; it will bring terrible fortune. And if you see the new moon through the trees you will have little money until the next one appears. Always pick a spot where you can see the crescent clearly without obstruction of vision. If you look over your left shoulder at any moon you will counteract bad luck. As long as the moon can be seen, you'll need to turn your back to it and your head to the left and peer straight into its glow.

Sprinkling salt into a sick person's bed will draw out soreness. (I might add that it is also uncomfortable for the patient.) It was done to my invalid mother by one of her sitters who firmly believed she was helping. Poor Mother thought she was lying on the beach. Her whole bed had to be changed and she was given a good bath.

The children in my town picked up a variety of charms during my day. For example, we'd blow a kiss or stamp our fist when we saw a gray mule. This would allow us either luck or a wish that was sure to come true. One of our favorites: When you cross a railroad track, be sure to hold up your feet. If not, your luck will run down the tracks.

Last summer, my childhood friend, Elizabeth (Mathis) Cheatham and I were on a bus trip to visit the national parks in the West. Every time we would reach a track we'd scream out, "Hold up your feet for luck!" This became a trademark for us, but the entire group began to enjoy these crossings and our little superstition. They would even spot the tracks before we did and warn the others.

Many of you will remember "If you step on a crack you'll break your mother's back." Do you also cross your fingers when passing a cemetery? The same act with fingers is recommended if passing a funeral procession. If not you might soon be the dead one yourself. The children in my era believed these things to be true. And, did you know it is ill fate to take salt from another person's hand? Always have them put it down for you to pick up yourself.

Whether taken seriously or not, these sayings or beliefs have brought much pleasure to many people. There must be thousands more, and I'll surely kick myself for not mentioning many that simply won't come to my mind at this point. As soon as I see myself crossing fingers, or stamping my fist, I'll most likely be reminded of more.

I hope all of you will be careful about these ideas. Remember that I have given you ways to curtail some ill fortune through these old beliefs. I'm sure they will work for you too. Hope you enjoy these family recipes suitable for luck on January first.

Cracklin' Bread

1 cup cracklings
3 cups cornmeal, sifted
1 teaspoon salt
Water

Mash or break cracklings into small pieces. Pour 1/2 cup hot water over them. Pour this into meal. Add enough cold water to mix into stiff dough. Add salt and blend well. Let stand a few minutes before shaping. If too stiff, add more water. Form into small pones or little, flat loaves. Arrange on a well greased flat griddle or pan. (Bacon fat is desirable for coating.) Put in 400 degree oven. When slightly brown on top, reduce heat to 350 degrees and bake for 30 minutes or until well done through center. Pones will be crusty on outside and firm in centers. During first part of baking time, put container on top shelf of oven. When heat is changed, move to lower cooking area. Makes 8 to 10 pones depending on amount of dough used for pones.

Southern Collard Greens

1 large bunch of collard greens
1/2 pound ham hock or streak o-lean salt pork
Salt and a little sugar to taste
Water for boiling

Wash greens thoroughly. Strip from heavy center stalks and veins. Tear into small pieces. Place in a large pot. Cover with water. Wipe meat clean and add to greens. Season with salt and sugar. Cook over very low heat on top of stove for at least 2 hours or until very tender. Greens should be kept well under water throughout cooking period. Add more if needed. Correct seasonings. Drain and serve with meat taken from bone or slice the salt pork.

Delicious with hot pepper and vinegar sauce. Corn bread of some type is almost essential with this boiled vegetable. Many southerners enjoy the "pot lik'ker" or broth along with the greens and bread for dunking.

New Year's Day, when I was growing up, was nothing really special. My parents didn't go out on the eve of the day and my sister Leila and I were just put to bed at the normal time. The next day we would be greeted with, "Happy New Year, girls. It's a brand new year since yesterday." It didn't make much sense to me, but if my parents said it, I knew it was true.

Of course, we had the traditional hog jowl and peas, but not collards. Of course the peas are copper pennies denoting riches for the year and the jowl was for peace and happiness. Our peas were served on rice, not cooked with it, and the meat was boiled in the peas. I thoroughly disliked that slick, fat jowl, but was always encouraged to have just a little piece to be rewarded throughout the year with the good it represented.

Our family usually had broiled ham or sausage on the side along with corn bread in some fashion, cole slaw and sweet potatoes, which were almost always on our winter dining tables. There were always some sweets left from Christmas for dessert. I don't remember the extras, but surely there were expected ones on the first day of the brand new year.

Prior to the New Year and shortly after Christmas the Hookses, or paternal side of my family, always met together at Uncle Tommy and Aunt Ethel's home out in the country for a post-seasonal supper. It was a large and happy gathering. The "grown-ups" enjoyed the meal in the big dining room while the children were fed in the breakfast room prior to their parents' meal. It was much more fun for the youngsters this way.

Lights would be put on outside the house and the young ones would slide on hay stacks or play games until the meal was served. After we had eaten, we played games or created our own fun until time for the big event.

The great excitement came after we had all finished dinner. Each family would bring to the party the greatest amount of fireworks that Santa had delivered earlier in the week. They would be safely shot over a plowed field. The men in the family were responsible for firing them and we watched and cheered and exclaimed over their beauty. I do remember that sometimes Daddy would help me hold a Roman candle and let it go off in the sky above. But our parents were very careful with all of the children.

This great show would bring in neighbors who also enjoyed watching with us. There were five young Hooks cousins, Tommy III, George, Margaret, my sister Leila, and I and our youngest half-aunt, Nancy. It was a lively group and we all anticipated this after-Christmas event. George and I were the youngest and the same age. I recall his taking great pleasure in showing me his bird egg collection. He and his brother, Tommy, also had a goat and cart. If the weather was nice we would ride in it, but I associate that more with visits to their house later in the year.

All the female parents brought leftovers from Christmas for this Hooks meal. I do believe the host family provided a baked ham, but Mother carried turkey hash or creamed turkey and some sweets and the others provided similar delicacies. I don't know who was responsible for all the good food, but I do recall an abundance of homemade cakes and candies, to my extreme pleasure.

Before I give you recipes from this event, I must tell you a brief story. One time when we had gathered for the above entertainment Uncle Tommy told us that we were lucky to be there in his home. It had almost caught on fire and would have been completely demolished as the result of his boys stuffing the chimney with hay for Santa's reindeer. It was not discovered until a fire was built early the next morning. However, the flaming bundle was quickly extracted and snuffed out.

But two young boys were crying and said, "Why didn't Santa push the hay out and give it to his reindeer when he slid down the chimney? There must not be any Santa." But my quick-thinking uncle reassured them that the old man had chosen another chimney to use, yet found the stockings where they had been hung. Of course, he never bothered to check THAT chimney, but returned to the roof the way he had arrived. This satisfied not only his own sons, but all of his nieces as well. Because, of course, there IS a Santa! We all know that.

Now for some of the recipes we enjoyed at this post-Christmas gala. I think the cake was Grandmother Hooks' contribution since I know it was her youngest child's favorite. Mother made the hash or creamed turkey. Here are their recipes or similar ones.

Lemon Cheese Cake

1 cup butter
2 cups sugar
3 1/4 cups cake flour
2 teaspoons baking powder
1 cup milk
8 egg whites
1 teaspoon vanilla

Cream butter and sugar. Mix flour with baking powder. Add dry ingredients alternately with milk to first mixture. Fold in stiffly beaten egg whites. Add flavoring. Bake in 3 layers on ungreased, wax paper, lined pans at 350 degrees for 25 minutes or until cake tests done. Fill with following.

Filling

8 egg yolks
1 cup sugar
1/4 cup butter
3 large lemons, juice and grated rinds
White icing

Mix ingredients and cook in double boiler until it gels. Cool and spread on tops of all layers and top of cake. Put layers together and frost whole cake with desired white icing.

Turkey Hash

1 tablespoon minced onion
1/2 cup chopped celery
2 tablespoons butter
2 tablespoons flour
Broth from steamed turkey carcass, about 1 1/2 cups
3 cups cooked, chopped turkey
Salt and pepper to taste

Lightly saute onions and celery in butter. Remove cooked vegetables and add flour to pan. Stir briskly to a smooth paste. Slowly add broth, mixing well and stirring constantly. Add cooked turkey, onions and celery. Heat through. If too thick, add more broth or cream. Season to taste. Serve on toast strips or steamed rice to 10 to 12

It was usually during January that the big hog killings took place on the farms surrounding my home town in southwest Georgia. This was because hard freezes were likely to develop and that was the time that the meat could best be prepared and stored for future use. Deep freezers were not even imagined at that time, so preparation and storage of meat was an important consideration.

As weather predictions developed, I remember the phone ringing constantly in our house. It was always for Daddy. His father, his two brothers and most of his friends had farms and they needed to discuss the possibility of the big killing. Was it really going to be cold enough and stay that way for a few days? "What's the latest that you've heard about the weather?" was on most of the callers' tongues.

Once it was established that the mercury would truly drop into the teens, the plan was set. Daddy would call his overseer at the farm and tell him to get all the helpers together for the big morning. They would start very early and be dressed warmly. Quantities of wood and all the utensils were gathered and ready for use. The fires could be started, the receptacles cleaned and the tables set up and covered while the killing took place.

Daddy would get up before daybreak to go to the farm and start the procedure. He felt it was very necessary to be there as early as the rest of the crew. Mother joined him and the other workers after she got my sister and me off to school.

Large, long tables were set up outdoors with white oil cloth coverings. This material could be easily washed off after each job. Large fires were built throughout the area to keep the workers warm. Hot water was essential in keeping everything washed and clean. One tremendous long, hog tub was filled with water for boiling and used to remove the bristles from the pigs once they were killed and ready to be sectioned. These prickly hairs were the only part of the hog that was not edible.

When school was out, Leila and I would be picked up and taken to the nearby farm to see all of the action that we had anticipated following the many phone calls we'd overheard predicting the time for this event. Mother would be aproned in a huge white coverlet just like the other women who were working. She would have a woolen scarf tied over her head and heavy rubber gloves on her hands. She looked very unlike the beautiful, well-dressed Mama to whom we were accustomed. But she would be working happily right along with the rest of the people.

This was a big work day that would benefit our family, and all of the ones working, for days to come. Various parts of the animals would have been cut and lying out on the tables. Some of them were heavily salted for storage. Others would be portioned for use in the coming days. They had to be kept extremely cold, but generally these freezes lasted for several days, just as they do now, and the meat was readily usable.

Mother's speciality was making sausage. The scraps of good meat would be placed in front of her. There was a big grinder that she used with the help of other women on the farm. Ground meat, mixed with what spices she used, would be pressed into the long pieces of casing and stuffed evenly.

I wish that I had her recipe for this delicacy, but I don't. It was marvelous and the only sausage I ever tasted that was even comparable was made by other country-farm recipes.

Souse meat, or head cheese, was made from tiny scraps of meat cooked from the bones of the animals. Naturally there were hams, shoulders, backbones, ribs, bacon and side meat or fat back. The lard was rendered in a large pot over a huge fire. Although the weather was frigid, the many open fires gave everybody working an opportunity to leave their posts and warm up from time to time.

Daddy was supervisor of the operation and seemed to be everywhere. He would joke with the workers and also chop or cut right along with them. His gentle manner seemed to spark the day and everybody was willing to work hard. Of course, the rewards were many, for nobody went home empty handed of meat or pay.

I can remember seeing the salted hams and meats being taken to the smoke house where they were cured. Here meat could be held through warmer weather. We always referred to these hams as "country" ones.

Chittlings and the brains were not to our liking, and others who relished them made bids for their share. I don't recall that we were ever served the liver, which I now think is delicious. But we truly had our share of fresh pork meat after the big kill.

Mother would be full ready to return home shortly after her children arrived and I don't wonder. She was a good sport to help and it was not normal work for her. I'm sure the cold weather was objectionable too. But she was not different from the other wives of people who had farms and who also worked on these particularly cold days.

Once the lard was rendered, it was poured into large, airtight buckets and distributed. The small pieces of fat that had not melted away were put aside for that wonderful crackling bread. My, what good eating lay ahead for all of us.

The fresh meat was taken home and refrigerated as the weather changed. In our house was a cold pantry, and that is where Mother would hang long pieces of sausage to let them dry out slightly. Much of the fresh meat could be kept on shelves in there, too, until the weather changed. I don't remember ever having smoked sausage from our farm, but I surely did like the fresh and still do. What a blessing we didn't know about cholesterol at that time.

Does it sound strange to think that children would anticipate and truly enjoy the big days of hog killing? We were spared the bloody part and had fun watching the different workers at their skills. If we got tired of watching, we might join the farm children, jump rope together or slide on hay. They taught us some of their own games, which was fun.

Before I give you any recipes let me say that one of the most beautiful parts of such a hard working day was the beautiful singing that accompanied it. I can hear those lovely voices as I write, singing mostly church hymns, as they worked at their tasks. I truly feel that I have been a most fortunate person to have had such a variety of interesting experiences as I grew up.

Now for some of the recipes.

Backbone With Dumplings

Fresh pork backbone
Boiling water to half cover meat
Salt and black pepper to taste
Dumplings:
2 cups flour
4 teaspoons baking powder
1 teaspoon salt
1 cup milk

Cut backbone into serving size pieces. Wipe with a damp cloth or paper towel. In a large pot, cover up to half with boiling water. Add salt and pepper and bring to a boil. Reduce heat, simmer for about 2 hours or until thoroughly tender. Add water if broth becomes too low.

Make dumplings by mixing all ingredients together. Flour hands and form into pieces about the size of a walnut. Drop into boiling pot and cook about 10 minutes. Do not stir. Cover and boil rapidly for a few minutes. Dumplings will rise to top and be light and fluffy if cover is not removed during this brief boiling period. Serve at once with mixture of meat and dumplings.

Remember, former cooks had large, wood-burning stoves which were very good for slow simmering. This made the meat very tender and dumplings light.

Souse Meat or Head Cheese

1 small hog's head
5 to 6 pig's feet
Water to half cover meat
1 hot pepper pod, cut fine
1 tablespoon pulverized sage
Salt and pepper to taste

Remove brains and nose of pig. Wash, scrape, and singe the head and feet until thoroughly clean. Put them over low heat in hot water adding hot pepper. Cook slowly until the meat falls from bones. Pick or cut this meat into fine bits and work in salt, pepper and sage. (This is most often done by hand.)

Pack in a stone jar and put in a cool place. It will congeal. When cold, hold the jar over hot water for a few minutes and the cake will turn out whole. It will slice nicely and is delicious cold with hot grits as an accompaniment or as a sandwich meat. Refrigerate leftovers.

 *Magical Nights*

Winter nights were great fun in our neighborhood. Those of us who grew up on Harrold Avenue in Americus were all very congenial. We created games for one, two or three persons or a large group. While we mostly played on our own, there were some winter nights that stand out in my memory.

My parents, Glenn and Clara Belle Davenport Hooks, were both young and participated in many of our activities. In fact, they encouraged us. Looking back, our little bungalow-type house was the center of a majority of these gatherings. In the summer our wide front porch made a fine play area and in the winter friends were welcomed into the house for fun evenings.

Always, during the winter, there would be a Friday night when Daddy would tell Leila and me to invite anybody who wanted to join us to see him "pin a glass of water" to the wall. This feat naturally intrigued our friends. Nobody could imagine how in the world a glass filled with water could be pinned to a flat wall. It seemed magic enough just to pin an empty glass.

After everybody arrived and anxiously awaited the magical trick, Daddy would pour water into a glass from a pitcher. He would say that the trick would require a good sport to hold onto the tumbler while he carefully attached it to the wall. Many volunteers would clamor forth. He would carefully look each one over. Sometimes he would even ask to feel their muscles since it might require strength to hold the receptacle in place.

Once the selection was made the holder was asked to approach the wall with him. Together they would decide on a spot where he would pin the water-filled glass. Next he asked Mama to produce a straight pin. Then the volunteer was instructed to hold the glass tightly against the wall. Daddy held the pin tightly and placed it next to the glass.

At this point he would drop the pin on the floor. As he, Mama and the volunteer looked around for it he would dribble a little water on the good sport making all of us laugh. Of course, we realized it was impossible to attach a hard container to the house with a small pin. But it never failed to promote amusement.

He would highly praise the brave person who had been lightly sprinkled and we all clapped for him or her. Naturally this could be done only once for most of us since we already knew the trick. But when new friends came into the neighborhood the whole group would return to see this fun sport. Nobody ever seemed to mind being "it."

Another of his magic tricks which he performed on the same night included either Leila or me. Before our guests arrived he would take one of us to the kitchen. There, with a cake of soap, he'd draw our initials on an arm. This was to be kept very secret. The colorless soap could not be detected.

At the given time he would tell the group that he could make letters appear on a person's arm with a piece of burned paper. Everybody wanted to be "the person" and he patiently helped several roll up sleeves as he rubbed a sooty mess over their arms. No letters were seen. Finally, the child who had been previously soaped would come forward and well-formed letters appeared over the prepared area.

Everybody would appear astonished and beg to be rubbed with charred paper. But after the trick ended he would not dirty other guests. He'd most often explain that only one person had the ability to perform such magic.

Mama patiently washed the dirty little arms of our friends before pulling down their sleeves. We never told anybody how the stunt was accomplished.

This might be a fun little game with a group of younger children. It doesn't need to make a mess, either, since newspapers can be placed on the floor under the area where the rubbing will take place. Then they can be carefully removed and the floor tidied.

After a winter indoor night of games, Mama always gave us light refreshments. We either had spiced cider and cookies or hot chocolate. I have selected some of her recipes that pleased our group.

Spiced Cider

1/2 teaspoon whole cloves
1/2 teaspoon whole allspice
6 inches stick cinnamon, broken, or to taste
1 quart apple cider
1/4 cup sugar
Juice of 1/2 lemon

Place spices in a piece of cheese cloth and tightly tie top to forn a bag. Heat cider with sugar. Add spices and allow to come to a boil. Boil 5 minutes, remove from heat and add lemon juice. Serve hot. Makes 12 tea cup servings. Note: A tea ball may be used for holding the spices if desired,

Oatmeal Macaroons

2 tablespoons butter
1 cup granulated sugar
2 eggs, beaten
1 teaspooon almond or vanilla extract
2 1/2 cups rolled oats
1 teaspoon baking powder
1/4 teaspoon salt

Soften butter slightly. Add sugar and eggs. Fold in flavoring. Mix oats, baking powder and salt. Add to first mixture. Drop by spoonful on greased baking sheets. Bake at 400 degrees for 12 minutes or until lightly brown on tops and around edges. Makes a large quantity, depending on amount dropped from spoon. Mama considered these very healthy.

I've written about some of the simple pleasures we enjoyed as games when I was growing up. My parents were always taking part in the activities that they had played as children.

One, that many of you have may have played, was "Spin the Pan." I well remember the rug being turned back in our living room for this game. It is best accomplished on a hard floor.

The equipment needed is a pie pan, tin or aluminum. A wide floor area is essential. It is also necessary to have several good friends participating. In fact, the more, the merrier, as the old saying goes.

Players sit in a circle. After selecting the first "it" that person moves to the center of the ring. He or she must then take the pan, stand it on one end and twirl it hard. The more it twirls, the better.

The spinner must call the name of a person in the circle who should quickly hop up and grab the utensil before it stops twirling. If that player misses and the pan falls to the floor then a pawn is paid by the loser, and he/she gets the next turn to spin.

Pawns were something we could identify as our very own when it came time to be reclaimed. Girls used hair ribbons, clips, bracelets or anything quickly available. Boys handed over marbles, pocket knives, handkerchiefs, neckties or the like. It was important to have many pawns on hand for retrieving at the conclusion of the sport.

The one called to the center was then allowed to spin the pan and invite another friend to try to catch the pan. We found out very quickly that if we hesitated about calling a name that it was more difficult for the catcher to reach the center. Once every person in the circle had been called and turned in at least one personal object the spinning part of the game ended.

Since my parents took part in most of these home entertainments, they were the ones to work with the pawns. Now it was time for all of the players to take their original seats in the circle. We faced the grown ups. One older person would be seated and the other standing behind the chair in order to be unseen. The standing adult would say to the seated one. "I am holding an interesting pawn to be returned." (This would bring giggles from the players for we'd know to whom the object being held belonged.)

Next the seated partner would say to the person holding the unseen pawn, "Is it fine or super fine?" "Fine" objects belonged to the boys, and "super fine" to the girls. This gave the adult in the chair a clue. Once the male or female identity was known the seated person would say, "Would the boy/girl who owns this object please stand?"

Each child had to perform a stunt in order to have the object being held returned. Upon seeing who it was, directions were given by the adult for the type stunt to be executed. This seemed a fair way taking into consideration the age and skill of the child.

Among the feats requested might have been to recite a nursery rhyme or say a short verse. Little songs were also popular, and twirling around three times or doing a somersault might have been another. The adults selected a stunt that could be accomplished by the child. After the tricks were completed, the players got back their treasures.

If there were only six or eight children, there was probably time to enjoy a second round. But on our Harrold Avenue, when the neighbor children were invited for this type of entertainment they arrived in bunches. So usually time allowed only a single game.

Leila and I felt very popular to know that all the children liked to come to our house for game nights. Little did we realize that the attraction was not our own charm. Mother and Daddy, taking part in all of these activities, were the major winning point. After I was grown one of my friends confessed to me that she always liked to visit my sister and me. But she added, "It was your parents that I really adored."

I'm completely amazed, at this point in life, that my Hooks parents spent so much time with us and our friends. Mama even went the extra mile by serving some of her delicious cookies and a beverage to the group. If she'd had a busy day, "store-bought" treats were passed around. Nobody ever left without a tasty treat.

Both my parents were very sensitive to children's feelings. They would do anything to keep from embarrassing or hurting one. It was a lesson they passed on to my sister and me. I hope I have been able to follow their example. I have earnestly tried. These recipes were often served at one of the events.

Dropped Cookies

1/2 cup shortening
1 cup sugar
2 eggs, well beaten
1/2 cup milk
1/2 cup molasses or cane syrup
3/4 cup currants or raisins
3/4 cup chopped pecans
3 cups flour
3 level teaspoons baking powder
1 level teaspoon cinnamon
1/2 level teaspoon ground cloves

Cream shortening and sugar. Add eggs and mix well. Combine milk, molasses, raisins and nuts to first mixture. Sift together dry ingredients and mix them in last. Drop by spoonful on greased tins some distance apart since they will spread while cooking. Bake 10 minutes or until lightly browned on tops at 350 degrees. Makes a large quantity.

Chocolate Cookies

1/2 cup butter
1 cup sugar
1 egg
2 squares chocolate, melted
1/4 cup milk
2 cups flour
1/3 level teaspoon salt
1 1/2 level teaspoons baking powder

Cream butter and sugar. Add egg, melted chocolate and milk. Sift together flour, salt and baking powder. Add to other ingredients. Roll out thinly, about 1/4-inch thick, on floured surface. Cut into rounds or desired shapes. Bake on greased pans at 400 degrees for 10 minutes.

Transportation Ideas

Bear with me for one more old-fashioned game. Remember, when my parents were growing up they didn't have the advantage of many of the toys and equipment my sister and I had. They were taught these fun sports by their own parents, so I do feel these entertainments are significant.

My parents' parents played with the children, which always made the game more fun. My father said one of his most pleasant memories of his mother, who died at age 26, was joining the children in their games.

So here goes for one of those long-ago treasures that I have taught to many families who seem to enjoy it with their children, too. The title of it is "William, William Trimble Toe." Any number can play. The players sit in a circle on the floor, except one, usually a parent. This designated person is the counter or leader. The players put their fists on the floor with their index fingers extended.

The counter begins by touching all of the children's fingers as he/she says the following, each word spoken represents one index finger touched:

William, William Trimble Toe,
He's a good fisherman
Catches hens, puts them in pens,
Some lay eggs, some none,
Wire, briar; nimble nock
Set and sing 'till 6 o'clock,
Clock runs down,
Mouse runs round
O-U-T spells out and out you go,
To old dirty dish rag's house.

When the last finger is touched with the final word, that player is required to leave the play area. When our Hooks family taught this in Americus to our Harrold Avenue friends Daddy was usually the counter.

He would often stretch out the last words passing quickly over some small fingers in order to end on an older child's hand. He felt the more mature players would be better subjects to leave the room.

When the selection was made that person would temporarily be dismissed from the play area. Mama would often accompany the lone child to a nearby room so no one felt left out or afraid.

While the outside person was awaiting orders from the leader of the game, those still in the circle named an animal or object they thought the dismissed person would not like to ride. We came up with imaginative ideas like snakes, pigs and so forth for ourselves hoping that they would not be selected.

Then the leader invited the dismissed one back by listing all the choices we in the circle had offered. The person whose suggestion was taken by the loner would be responsible to bring him/her back into the room. The dismissed child was either carried or given a piggy-back ride.

But there was an extra fun trick in all of this. The group could choose a mode of transportation on which they thought the dismissed person would like to ride. We all tried hard to think of what that individual would most possibly prefer.

If this were the case then the loner would have to return to the group on his own. This was announced by saying, "Come back on your tip toes," which we took seriously and balanced ourselves back to the play area heels up.

Most of us would think of dreadful rides, animals and broken-down vehicles for ourselves. We'd then choose a shining car, airplane, white circus pony or something of the sort for the dismissed player. Nobody wanted to have to haul their friend back into the room.

Once all decisions had been made, the counter would call to the other room and say, "When are you coming home?" Answer, "Tomorrow afternoon." Question, "What are you going to bring?" Answer, "A dish, a spoon and a fat raccoon."

The retriever would then ask the returned child which would be preferred to be dropped on, a feather bed or one of nails. Naturally, first-time players would select the soft choice. But if they selected the soft choice of the feather bed, the counter would then say, "Put the rider down HARD" because the bed is soft. Had the answer been the nails, the rider would be put down easily and carefully. This never failed to bring much laughter.

It is not a long game and could be played several times in an evening, depending on the number involved. It was and is fascinating to hear what the various youngsters would come up with for ideas of rides.

In these modern times the ride choices could be really wild. But when we were playing it was simpler with a variety of animals, bikes, wagons, cars, wheelbarrows, trains and even street cars.

There's something that makes us feel good to pass on these old ideas to a new generation. And especially since our youngsters are becoming so sophisticated. They also now have such outlandish toys and equipment for playing. But if parents will just play this with them, you will no doubt see great enthusiasm from your computer-oriented children. We all liked these recipes.

Our Favorite Pineapple and Cheese Sandwiches

2 white bread slices, cut round
1 round slice canned pineapple, drained and patted dry
A hearty sprinkling of sharp, grated cheese
Mayonnaise for spreading

Cut bread slices round, just a little wider than the pineapple slice. Cover both slices with mayonnaise. Place prepared pineapple on one covered side, sprinkle with cheese and put top layer, mayonnaise side down, over all. Serve at once. These do not keep well.

Deviled Egg and Bacon Sandwiches

6 hard-boiled eggs
6 slices crisp bacon, crumbled
1 tablespoon sweet or dill pickle relish
1 teaspoon prepared mustard
Salt and pepper to taste
Mayonnaise to make spreading consistency

Put cooked eggs through food chopper or mash well with fork. Add remaining ingredients. Mayonnaise should be last addition and only enough to make mixture smooth for spreading. Use on whole wheat or white bread slices.

Valentine's Day was always a special time at our school and in the neighborhood. A large container, or Valentine's box, was placed in the front of the classroom about a week before. It was highly decorated with crepe paper fluffs, solid red valentines, lacey hearts and red streamers.

Once my friend, Martha, and I had the rare opportunity of covering one for our class. Boy, did we feel important. It must have taken us hours to prepare. Our mothers gave us little scraps of real lace and ribbons for it. We were sure that it was the finest one ever.

We began bringing Valentines to school as soon as the large container appeared and awaited the important time when it would be opened and the contents distributed. This was always done at the very end of Valentine's Day and must have taken well over an hour. We felt so special when our names were called and we would walk up to get our prize.

Many of us always gave one to everybody in our class and, of course, a special one for the teacher. It was an exciting day to see how many we would receive since some of us were given more than just one by our friends. Martha and I always gave each other several in order to be assured of quantity. My sister, Leila, also put some in the box in my room, when she was still at the same school. Naturally, I returned the favor.

Our valentines were seldom "store bought." Not only were those expensive, but also we took great pleasure in making our own. In order to prepare our beauties we usually sat on the floor in front of our open fire. We made paste of flour and a little water. Remember, we didn't have bottles of glue or sticky tape in those days. But this worked well. We also found that egg whites were sticky and could be used, but the flour paste, prepared in a little saucer, was usually our choice.

Our art teacher at school helped us make special valentines we usually gave to parents and grandparents. There we had the advantage of real glue. It was passed around to our desks and taken from a large jar. Each student had an ink well on the desk that contained a small cup or jar. The glue was poured into the ink well. We applied it with a little wooden paddle similar to a tongue depressor.

After preparing these at school the whole class was usually pretty sticky from the use of glue. While it was a joy for us, I'm certain that it must have been a horror for our regular teachers.

On Valentine's night the children in our neighborhood would call on friends and toss their cards on the front porches. We used broom sticks to rap on the floors of the chosen houses after the valentines had been thrown. Then we'd hide.

All of our cards for home and school were signed "guess who" instead of using names. The fun was trying to figure out who left cards for us. We would try to find an almost hidden place on the valentine where we could put our initials in little secret places. This, of course, would be a clue for the receiver and made guessing easier.

Leila and I would hide near the front door and peek out when we heard the banging on our porch. Often we would hear callers coming toward our home. We were ready to try to catch them when and if they visited us. It was actually more fun not to catch them, but there were times when we just couldn't help ourselves.

I truly hope there are Valentine boxes in the schools today. My children had bags that they decorated and placed on the sides of their desks for receiving cards. That wasn't half as much fun. There was never street delivery for my youngsters either. What a pity!

Here now are some of the recipes that were appropriate for the big day.

Aunt Florence's Tea Cakes

1 1/2 cups sugar
1/4 cup lard
3/4 cup butter
4 eggs
1 quart sifted plain flour (about 3 and 1/5 cups)
2 teaspoons cream of tartar
1 level teaspoon soda
1 teaspoon vanilla

Cream butter, lard and sugar until fluffy. Beat in eggs one at a time with vanilla. Sift dry ingredients. Work into stiff dough. Roll very thin on floured board. Cut in heart or desired shapes. Bake at 350 degrees for about 10 to 12 minutes or until lightly brown. Cool and store in air-tight containers. Makes 6 to 7 dozen, round, 2-inch cookies. Heart shaped ones may be a little larger so fewer would be the yield. These freeze well.(This is such an old recipe that I still weigh my sifted flour in order not to vary the original.)

Strawberry Congealed Salad

3 1/2 cups frozen or fresh, sliced strawberries
1/2 cup whipped cream
2 oranges peeled and cut into sections, membranes removed
1/2 cup chopped pecans
Juice of 1 lemon
1 package, 3 ounce size, strawberry flavored gelatin

Make packaged gelatin by directions on box. When chilled to white of egg consistency, add fruits and nuts along with lemon juice. Fold in whipped cream. Pour into heart shaped mold or individual ones for Valentine's Day. Makes 10 to 12 servings.

Southern Biscuits

2 1/2 cups flour
3 teaspoons baking powder
1 teaspoon salt
1/2 cup lard or shortening
3/4 cup sweet milk

Heat oven to 450 degrees. Mix the dry ingredients and cut in shortening until mixture resembles peas. Stir in milk mixing well. Round up the dough on a lightly floured board. Knead very lightly. Roll out to about 1/2-inch thickness. Cut in rounds and place on ungreased cookie sheet. Bake for 10 to 12 minutes. Makes about 20 and should be served with plenty of butter and very hot. Buttermilk may be substituted for regular milk if desired. If so, reduce baking powder to only 2 teaspoons and add 1/2 teaspoon soda and 2 more tablespoons shortening. These should be rolled out more thinly. Mother used what ever sort of milk she had on hand.

# Birthday Parties

February may be the shortest of our twelve months, but it is the fullest with birthdays in my family. Mine is also this month and it started me to thinking about the birthday parties that we had as children. We played little ring games like "Drop the Handkerchief," "Many, Many Stars," "Go in and Out the Windows," and others of that type. We also pinned the tail on the donkey and I remember "Blind Man's Bluff" as another favorite.

I hate to lose these little games in our lives and have been delighted to teach some of them to the kindergarten children at my church and similar gatherings. The children seem to enjoy them as much as we did and it delights me unceasingly to watch their pleasure while playing.

The children attending our parties assembled in their Sunday clothes. They would come bearing inexpensive gifts carefully wrapped in tissue paper and tied with real satin ribbons.

Age made little difference at our parties. All cousins were usually invited to mine and my sister Leila's. We had two older half aunts who came to our celebrations. Naturally, our close friends and neighborhood buddies were invited with no discrimination about boys and girls.

After playing games for a short time we would be invited into the dining room of the honoree's house. There was always a canopy of crepe paper streamers attached from the chandelier over the center of the table to the edges where we stood. We were usually placed between the ribbons and all the way around the table where we awaited our refreshments. The honoree was given the most prominent location.

Many children chose to have a variety of colors for their canopy, but Leila and I always wanted just pink. I have come to associate this color with birthdays and still wrap my sister's annual gift in pink paper.

My maternal grandmother, Leila Crisp Davenport, lived across town from us and usually made the birthday cakes for my sister and me. This way we had no opportunity of seeing them until our big day.

Our cakes were baked with certain common tokens in them. There was a thoroughly scrubbed dime, a thimble or button and sometimes an inexpensive little ring baked into the batter. The person who received the coin was designated to become rich. The button or thimble meant spinster or bachelorhood. As I recall, the thimble was for a female and the button for a boy. Naturally the winner of the ring would be the first to be married.

Each child was given a paper hat to wear. They came in a variety of colors but looked very much like the ones that can be made out of a newspaper, with turned up edges and a point on top. Little tiny paper cups were put at our places to be a treat for all. The containers were highly decorated with pleated crepe paper skirts or ruffles around them. Some had handles and others were just plain. They were filled with hard candies and we were urged to take them home with us.

We were served homemade ice cream in cones, regardless of the weather. It was boiled custard type at our house and most often at others too.

Our cakes were always frosted heavily, but there were no decorations as we see today. Nor were there special themes for our parties. We very simply celebrated our day in similar fashion from home to home. There was something comforting about the similarities of all of them. There was no trying to be the greatest or the least. It was just a nice gathering with delicious treats.

Fancy favors were not given the guests except the paper hats and candy cups. There were prizes if that type game was played and a winner declared. Never were they expensive gifts but just appropriate ones suitable for girls or boys of all ages.

Our gifts were held until the end of the party when everybody surrounded the honoree as the presents were opened. Each person was properly thanked for his or her contribution. All of us had been taught to politely thank the honoree and hostess mother upon leaving. I believe that we were taught very nice manners about everything and birthday parties were a time when it was quite evident.

As we grew older we had picture-show parties (or "movie" parties to our present generation). There were also skating ones. Summer birthdays could be swimming events followed by a watermelon cutting in addition to the usual cake and trimmings.

Now I am pleased to give you Mother's recipe for boiled custard ice cream which was part of our celebrations. The cones were purchased either at Mr. Sparks' Grocery or from a local drug store. Our cakes were One-Two-Three-Four ones made in three layers and heavily frosted between layers. on top and the sides.

The cake recipe has been printed often. I shall instead offer you a recipe that should be used during the holiday season. I'm giving the old fashioned version but since so many people are afraid of using raw eggs in recipes the boiled custard recipe may be substituted with similar success, according to my young friend, Damon Fowler, Savannah, author of *Classic Southern Cooking.*

Boiled Custard Ice Cream

Boiled custard:
1 cup sugar
4 eggs, well beaten
1 quart milk
1 teaspoon vanilla
Ice cream:
1 quart heavy cream
1 additional cup sugar

Mix beaten eggs and sugar. Add milk, mixing well. Place in top of double boiler over very hot water. Stir constantly until mixture thickens and is smooth and thick enough to coat a spoon. Cool and add vanilla. Add the cream and extra sugar. Pour into freezer churn and freeze according to directions on churn.

When thoroughly stiff, remove dasher and pack with additional ice around covered container until time for use. Makes a little over 1/2 gallon.

Southern Eggnog

3 eggs
4 tablespoons sugar
6 tablespoons brandy, bourbon or your choice of whiskeys
1/2 cup whipping cream
Nutmeg for topping
Few grains of salt

Whip cream stiff and add 1 tablespoon of the sugar. Separate eggs. Beat whites stiff, using a separate bowl, adding remainder of sugar and salt slowly. Beat constantly until they hold a peak. Let stand while beating yolks. Beat yolks until light. Add liquor slowly stirring or whipping all the time. When well mixed, pour yolk mixture into whites folding in using an over and under motion. Never beat. Whipped cream may then be folded into mixture in the same manner. Pour into tall glasses accompanied by an iced tea spoon. Top with a sprinkling of nutmeg. Serve immediately to 3 or in smaller glasses to 6. (If using the boiled custard you will simply need to fold in the bourbon and whipped cream.)

I can remember my maternal grandmother Davenport, who usually supervised this Christmas special, saying to my father, who helped, "Glenn, add more whiskey to the egg yolks until they seem cooked." She actually felt that the strong liquor cooked the eggs, and perhaps it did. It never made any of my family ill. The children were never given this treat. We had syllabub flavored with vanilla as a substitute.

For the most part I have written almost entirely about the pleasant happenings during my growing-up days. I now want to tell you about a long illness that I had and the way contagious diseases were treated years ago. I remember coming home from school one winter afternoon and telling Mama that I felt awful. She took one look at me and said I had flushed cheeks. She took my temperature. I had a fever, so she tucked me in bed.

By the time Daddy came home from work that night the fever had risen. They asked many questions. Did my throat feel sore? Did I ache anywhere? Did my tummy hurt? Had I been sneezing often? And always, with any sickness, we were told to poke out our tongues. Apparently, this designated a stomach disorder if there was a white coating on this portion of the anatomy.

"I just hurt all over," I remember telling them.

This prompted a call to our family physician, Dr. J. W. Chambliss. He came over to our little Harrold Avenue house, examined me from head to toe and pronounced that I could be coming down with little red measles, which was prevalent all over town then. My sister, Leila, had already had this disease, but I hadn't, so it was possible.

My parents were told to look for a rash within a day or so and when or if it developed to call him back. I think it was the next day that I became splotchy with an itchy skin irritation. By the time the doctor came back to my house I must have been the color of a strawberry. "No doubt about it now," he said. "I must put up the precaution sign."

That announcement made me sicker than I had been, for I knew about the red sign. It always bore large black letters of warning, "Contagious Disease." My neighbor and classmate, Clarke Pool, had one of these signs on his house when he had scarlet fever. We even held our breath when we passed his house to avoid breathing any germs that might have emitted from it in our directions. All of the children had been told, with horror, that his disease was such a terrible one it would last for six

weeks. But the worst part was that all his old toys and bed clothes had to be burned. No germs were to linger in his home.

I burst into sobs when I heard a similar caution sign being hammered by my own front door. "Will you burn all of my toys too?" I asked.

I was told my contagion was not as serious as his, but I would be allowed to see only those persons who'd had measles. My own Hooks family rallied completely to me. Mama was ever protective and even closed the outside shutters on my room along with pulling down the green shades. Protecting the eyes from light was essential, she'd been told.

My case must have been a very severe one. I missed almost a month of school. I was not allowed out of bed or my room for over three weeks. I couldn't see my constant playmate and friend, Martha, but she brought our homework to her house for me. Lelia retrieved it.

Mama devoted most of her time to me. She sang songs, told me stories and would lie down beside me. We'd play "I Spy" selecting objects in the room that could be seen. One would choose and the other would guess. We took turns at being chooser and guesser.

We also played "Bum Ditty." Lying in bed on my side Mama would tap my back saying this little phrase. "Bum ditty, bum ditty, cows in the corn, how many fingers do I hold up?" I would guess the number and she would counter with, "Four, you said, but three it was." The game would continue until I was correct. Then Mama would be the guesser. If either of us missed, the same person would continue the tapping.

Leila would visit me after school. She told me about her day's experiences and how my friends inquired of my illness. When I was able to sit up in bed she played paper dolls with me.

Daddy's visits to my room would be filled with fairy tales and stories about his growing up on the farm. He also entertained me with Uncle Remus stories and little chants he knew as a child. He taught them to me along with other rhymes.

Grandmother Davenport came many days to relieve Mama. It must have been very difficult for my mother. I was not only to be kept quiet but both parents were also very concerned about my severe illness. All of this unselfish care was dear and I was well aware of the special attention I received.

I also worked on my school work. I learned the multiplication tables and spelling words, little poems and songs the class learned. These exercises did not require using my eyes and enabled me to keep up with some of the rest of my friends.

I had been back at school only about two days when report cards were distributed. I can remember the horror of seeing "No Report" on my card. I was a striver for all of the best marks, and felt that I had been mistreated.

When I came home almost in tears Mama explained the problem. It was simply because I had not been in classes enough days to be counted. She said she knew I would have my usual anticipated report the next month. After all, I was well up on spelling, multiplication, and all of the memory work.

While it was a long and unpleasant illness, I realize what a truly fortunate child I was to have enjoyed so much loving care. Mama told me I could be the one to take that horrid caution sign off of the house. That was pure joy.

These recipes were allowed following an illness.

Morie Fruit Salad

2 grapefruits, peeled and sectioned
6 oranges, peeled and sectioned
2 1/2 cups canned white cherries, drained
15 3/4 ounce can chopped pineapple, drained
4 envelopes or 4 tablespoons plain gelatin
1/2 teaspoon lemon juice
Dash of salt

Peel, section and remove all membranes from oranges and grapefruits. Cut into small pieces. Reserve juices. Drain canned fruits and add juices to fresh ones. Bring 3 cups of liquid to a boil. Pour over gelatin that has been soaked in 1 cup fruit juice. Water may be adddded if juices are not sufficient. Mix well to dissolve gelatin. Cool until the consistency of egg whites. Add all fruit and blend well. Pour into a large ring mold or individual ones. Refrigerate until firm. Unmold on lettuce leaves and top with a dollop of mayonnaise. Makes 16 to 20 servings.

Lime and Sour Cream Salad

1 (3-ounce) package lime flavored gelatin
1 cup hot water
1 1/2 cups crushed pineapple with juice
1 cup sour cream
1/2 cup chopped pecans

Dissolve gelatin in hot water. Chill until partially thickened. Add pineapple, nuts and cream. Cool until completely firm. Unmold on lettuce lined plates and top with mayonnaise.

Spring

Americus, Georgia, my birthplace, was well known, before my day and after, for its airport, Souther Field. It was there that pilots trained for World War I and later for World War II. It is still used as the landing field for my town as well as surrounding ones.

Souther Field was a place where we often flew kites during March's windy days. They were not store-bought, but we thought they were wonderful. Our father used newspapers to make them. We were especially pleased with one made from the colored funny papers. It was certainly more colorful to view.

He found lightweight sticks or thin wood for the frame that was tied together with light string. Then he and our mother would paste the covering over the sticks. Mama was ever ready with a nice tail for our kites. They were usually long pieces of sheets cut or torn into proper width and knotted along the way.

I remember many trials and errors before our great toy took flight. Other children were often out there too with their parents flying kites.

When Jimmy Carter was president this airport was constantly filled with planes and important people arriving for appointments with him. Many world-famous guests still come there to visit him when he is at his home in nearby Plains. One of the most distinctive characteristics of this field was that between the two world wars Charles Lindbergh used it to learn to fly. A plaque on the field commemorates this important feat.

I do not remember Mr. Lindbergh, though I was a little girl at the time. My father knew him since he often came to the auto garage Daddy, his father, and two older brothers owned. I well remember bringing in *The Macon Telegraph* bearing huge headlines announcing that memorable first non-stop flight across the Atlantic. My father was particularly excited and pleased.

I believe Mr. Lindbergh stayed at Mrs. Ketchum's boarding house. It was a very popular home for newcomers or singles. He lived in Americus only the few months that were required to complete his flight training. He was popular with my older relatives and friends. I've learned that he rode a motorcycle from St. Louis to Americus. I presume that he returned home in the same manner.

I am told that Souther is still the chosen spot for air shows. Vintage planes are often used for these events along with newer small aircraft.

I remember the airfield well from my childhood, since my father enjoyed visits out to this area on nice Sunday afternoons. Of course, he took along my mother and his two daughters if we wanted to go, which was most often the case.

A number of his young friends had bought airplanes and learned to pilot them. There was no doubt an active air school had located at Souther Field then.

The planes were probably the outdated ones that had been used in World War I. I remember they had two wide front wings that were separated and connected with what looked like heavy wires. I'm sure it must have been material of great strength, but how was I to know?

We must have been standing close to some of the planes when the pilots would take off. I remember Daddy calling out to them and they would respond. The propeller (I don't recall more than just one large one in the center front of the pilot's cabin) was large and strong. Once it began to turn it would blow dust and light gravel around. Mama always cautioned us to move way back in order to protect ourselves from the debris that was destined to fly.

Sometimes, when the pilots knew they had an audience, they would do flips and other stunts. It was very exciting for youngsters, as well as the adults. All would applaud and wave handkerchiefs to the pilots when they came close enough to view us. I don't think they ever soared extremely high in that day and time.

There was a day of horror connected to this field. One of the finest young men in town fell in a pine thicket on approach to Souther. He was preparing to land but fell too low and topped several trees that took him down. He was killed and his plane burned.

I remember riding out to see the damage, which was very close to the road that led to the field. It was extremely visible and caused me to

shudder when I saw it. He was a favorite friend of my parents, who were grief stricken about his untimely death.

But there are many good memories of the field, too. I well recall the beds of petunias that volunteered around some of the unused runways, which were concrete and looked like wide sidewalks. Leila and I would run around and pick a bouquet of these blossoms to take home.

This is certainly the month when the Glenn Hooks' family would have made many trips to Souther Field. March strongly reminds me of these delights.

The recipes included here were often served to us for a light supper after a visit to see the planes.

Cheese Souffle

1 cup medium white sauce (recipe follows)
1 cup very sharp cheese grated
4 eggs
1 teaspoon salt
1/8 teaspoon cayenne pepper

Make white sauce and remove from heat. Add grated cheese, salt and pepper. Mix well and let cool. Beat egg whites very stiff; set aside. Add slightly beaten egg yolks to the sauce. This will thin the mixture enough to pour over the beaten egg whites very gently. Fold in carefully to combine.

Pour mixture into a buttered baking dish and place dish in a pan of hot water. Place in preheated 350 degree oven and bake for 35 to 40 minutes. To test for donness, insert knife blade into center. If it comes out clean it is done. If it is sticky cook an additional 5 to 7 minutes. Serve at once on warm plates in order to avoid falling and becoming flat. Makes 4 servings.

Medium White Sauce

2 tablespoons butter
2 tablespoons flour
2 cups milk
1/4 teaspoon salt

Blend butter and flour over medium heat until a smooth paste is formed, stirring constantly. Gradually add milk and salt, stirring hard to avoid lumping. Stir constantly until smooth and thick. Turn heat off and cover to allow to cook an additional 5 minutes in its own heat. Thicker sauce is made with 3 tablespoons butter and flour and 3 cups milk. Thinner is reduced to 1 of each. Salt to taste.

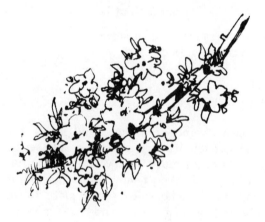

Easter Dresses Were
Gifts of Love

I always enjoyed Easter as a child. There were so many things that developed around this special day that I can't confine them to just one story. For now, I would like to tell you about our dresses.

Leila and I always had a dress made by Mama and Grandmother Davenport. Sometimes they worked on them together. Pattern books were purchased early. We scanned them to decide just what sort of dress we, and they, might like. Once the decision was made, the material had to be purchased with matching threads, trim and all that was necessary for the making of these garments.

I don't remember any of the mothers among my group of friends who didn't make clothes for their children. Every household had a sewing machine, and they were the rotary types. No electric ones were available at that time. These wonderful women pedaled and turned in order to provide special clothing for their sons and daughters.

If the Easter was a late one, our dresses might have been made of voile, organdy, pongee, or silk. Those were popular types of materials in my day. If it was an early holiday then we often felt stylish in an ensemble featuring a light weight woolen coat or jacket that coordinated with the lighter weight dress worn beneath.

I must have been about 5- or 6-years-old when when I was supplied with a pongee dress. We don't see this material often now, but I recall that it was silk-like and kind of beige in color.

Nobody might believe it to see me now, but I was a very thin child so my dresses were always made full. I recall that the pongee one was heavily smocked in bright colors to offset the neutral tone of the material. My mother and grandmother embroidered beautifully, but never smocked. This was usually done by a neighbor and close friend, Mrs. Ellis.

After the dress was cut out, the front and back were given to our friend for her needle work to be completed. Then my family sewers would put it together adding the sleeves, usually short ones with little cuffs, and a Peter-Pan type collar for this particular garment. It hung full from the smocking across the top of the chest and back. It was always exactly the correct length and fit for my frame.

All of this effort was done for us with tender, loving care. We greatly appreciated our new garments especially the Easter ones which were so special. Of course the school clothes were simple ones made of sturdy material and less adornment. However, the sewing machines hummed in most of the homes on my street constantly, but especially before Easter Sunday.

Now for some recipes that we enjoyed in our youth.

Banana bread

1/2 cup or 1 stick butter
1 cup sugar
2 eggs
2 cups flour
1 teaspoon baking powder
1 teaspoon baking soda
3 medium size bananas, fully ripe, mashed
Dash of salt
1 cup chopped nuts

Cream butter and sugar thoroughly. Add sugar gradually then the eggs, one at a time. Beat well and add the bananas that have been well mashed with a fork so there will be no lumps. Fold in flour, baking powder, soda, pinch of salt and nuts. Bake in greased loaf pan or pans at 300 degrees for about an hour, or until done. This recipe can also be made into muffins, if desired.

Lemon delight

1 (14-ounce) can cold evaporated milk
3 large juicy lemons
3 eggs, separated
Vanilla wafers
1 cup sugar

Beat egg yolks. Mix sugar and lemon juice and add to the yolks. Whip milk and fold into mixture. Fold in stiffly-beaten egg whites. In bottom of a refrigerator tray crumble a few vanilla wafers. Pour in the custard and crumble more vanilla wafers for topping. Use as many wafers as desired. (Mother used just a few.) Freeze for 6 hours or overnight. Cut into squares. This can be served just after refrigeration for an hour, but is especially good frozen during our hot months. Ours was usually topped with whipped cream.

With thoughts still on Easters of my past, you might be interested to know what a big event it was for us to purchase our new shoes for that special Sunday. Of course, they were also used for other special events until we outgrew them.

Once the dresses had been selected for me and Leila, my sister, it was necessary for us to get our new footwear. Mother generally bought her summer shoes at the same time. The three of us would ride to town in our little Model-T Ford or sometimes we would walk. It wasn't far from our house to downtown, and we enjoyed these excursions on pleasant days.

There was probably an additional shoe store to the one I remember, but Tillman & Brown's was the shop that we continually patronized. Walter Brown, one of the co-owners, lived only three houses away from us on Harrold Avenue in Americus. Mr. T.C. Tillman, whose first name I never knew because he was always addressed by his initials, lived only around the corner from our house. Naturally, my family enjoyed trading with our neighbors.

It was Mr. Walter who usually helped us. As I best remember, the men's and boys' shoes were on one side, and women's and girls' on the other.

I recall that the footwear was stacked on tall shelves all the way down the walls on both sides of the store. The stacks were so high that the men had sliding ladders on either side of the shop to reach the highest places.

It always seemed wonderful to me to watch those ladders slide down the walls. I remember asking if I could please climb up a few steps and Mr. Walter let me have a turn standing carefully behind me with his arms extended ready to catch me should I fall back. Of course, going to the top was out of the question, but I'd truly have liked that.

It was marvelous to see these nice men slide the ladder to its proper section, then climb up and bring down two or three boxes of shoes for us to try. If the fit was not correct nor the fashion to our liking, back up they would go, returning the first box to its proper place and then finding others.

Since I was the youngest, my needs were first filled. I was very tiny for my age and had a hard foot to fit, I was told. Once a pair was found I would try them on and walk around on the carpet to see if they felt right to me. My mother was ever so careful to be sure that the new foot dress was comfortable. Never were we allowed off the rug while sampling our choices. That would have scratched the bottoms of the slippers, making them seem worn. We were extremely careful to take the best care of these new slippers.

Mama and Leila would be trying on their choices as I strolled carefully around in mine. Wouldn't it be interesting to know what we paid for them in those days? I know what huge prices women's and children's shoes bring now. I have five grandsons, and I wonder how in the world their parents keep them well shod in this time of high costs.

We were always treated with special care at this shoe store. Our toes were pinched through the end of the slipper to be certain the shoes were not too tight. The salesmen were also careful to examine the heels as well in order to avoid rubbing against our skin and possibly forming a blister later.

Easter footwear was chosen for the summer months. Ours were generally white ones with a little strap across the top that buttoned on the opposite side. Sometimes there was cut-out trim on the top or sides. Often we received black patent leather; these could also be worn into the fall.

Most of the children whom I knew only had two pairs of shoes a year. One was for school, and they were laced-up brown ones. The others were the Sunday ones. As our "good" pair became roughed up or almost on the tight side, we were allowed to wear them to school. New shoes for everyday were purchased as we outgrew the old.

Sometimes, on the same day of getting new shoes, we also purchased our little straw hats for our outfits. This was not always the case because we could still wear the old ones. As in most families' circumstances, being the younger one in mine, I had Leila's hand downs. But they were always cleaned, and trimmed with fresh adornments so I was quite happy with any accessory that came my way.

After our shopping we always stopped by the drug store to buy ice cream cones. They only cost a nickel (buffalo-head type), and Leila and I would lick them all the way home. And what fun it was to show off our selections to Daddy when he came in that night.

Now for some more favorite recipes prepared in the Hooks home during those happy times.

Old-fashioned Cream Pie

2 cups milk
1/2 cup sugar
2 tablespoons flour
1/4 teaspoon salt
2 tablespoons butter
2 egg yolks
2 egg whites beaten stiff

Heat milk to hot, but not boiling. Mix sugar, flour, butter and salt together until creamy. Add egg yolks and beat until all is well blended. Slowly pour hot milk into this mixture until all is thoroughly mixed. Pour a small amount over stiffly beaten egg whites and then fold this well into the rest of the milk mixture. Pour into a 9- or 10-inch unbaked pie shell and bake at 400 degrees for 10 minutes. Lower the heat to 325 and bake about 25 minutes or until crust is brown and center tests done.

Pastry Shell

2 cups sifted all-purpose flour
1 teaspoon salt
3/4 cup vegetable shortening or lard
4 to 5 tablespoons ice water

Sift flour and salt together. Cut shortening into flour with pastry blender or 2 knives until mixture looks like crumbs. Sprinkle water over flour. Toss together to make a stiff dough. Chill for about 1 hour before rolling out on a lightly flour-coated pastry board or surface. Do not knead. Makes 2 pie shells, 8 to 9 inches each, or 12 tarts.

Back when cars were few, my Glenn Hooks family was fortunate to have a Model-T Ford. Daddy had farms and needed quicker transportation than we might have had by horse and buggy. We never had one of those, but I saw plenty in my day. I even had opportunities to ride in some that belonged to friends. Mama learned to drive our car, too, and both of my parents were generous about giving rides to those who were without automobiles. We could always scrunch over and make room for extra people to accompany us. Or, sometimes, they would take people to doctors for appointments or emergencies.

Not only did my family have a car but so did all of the Hooks farmers. My grandfather, Thomas Barden Hooks, had one of the first automobiles in our town. It was an electric one that I never saw, but I certainly heard about it from many older friends. That included my grandfather and Daddy's two brothers, J.D. and Tommy Hooks. They had farms, too, and at that period in life were able to afford these necessities. The Depression changed our financial statuses decidedly in later years. Another mode of transportation in my time in Americus, was street cars. I can't imagine why they were really needed because the town was small.

However, Lee Street did run a long way both north and south. Certainly there must have been many people who were unable to make the trip on foot. There was a section of town called Brooklyn Heights that was also further from the center of town. In addition, the east Americus settlement was some distance out, so I trust these were the families who rode the city transportation. The cost was only a nickel.

I can only remember riding them a few times just for the fun of it. These cars were later sold to the City of Macon and the tracks removed from our cobblestone streets before the streets were paved.

Traveling by car was not the grandest experience because of the roads. None of the country highways were paved and when it rained, believe me they were slick and sticky. Whenever we took a trip out of town during a wet season, we expected to get bogged down at least once and sometimes twice in a day.

Georgia is famous for its beautiful red clay, but it was also hazardous for traveling in my time. When the weather was dry, dust of the same bright hue would fly into our faces.

Ours was an open vehicle, however, and even the floors of the automobile would have particles of the surrounding dirt. If it was wet, we'd bring mud into the car on our feet. The lighter dust would just sift in as we rode. Some of it seemed always to be with us.

Mama always made us put Vaseline into and around our noses and lips in order to catch some of it. This was done for health reasons. After returning, from one of those dry day rides, we also were astonished to see how red our washcloths would be after scrubbing faces and hands clean. The rest of our bodies were better protected since we were enclosed somewhat in the car.

Those bad roads with deep ruts often resulted in unexpected flat tires. It wasn't a bit unusual to have TWO flats on a single trip. The spare tire could be used, but we had to have the bad one repaired before going any further. This could cause endless delays on longer trips. We knew of many accidents caused by slick roads and blow-outs which made drivers most cautious.

Fortunately, there were some paved roads connecting towns. When we'd drive for a visit to our Melton kin in Griffin, there were quite a bit of two-lane paved roads. But there were still many sections of clay highway.

I remember one visit up there when it took us eight hours to drive the 90-mile journey. We always had to stop for gasoline a couple of times, but there was a tire change on that excursion and also some engine trouble, a result of heavy rains. We had to telephone our relatives twice to explain our terrible delay.

My close friend, Elizabeth (Mathis) Cheatham, recalls how she was terrified many times on trips from Americus to the McDonough area. Her father drove the family to his wife's parents' home, which was on a big farm. This was an annual trek Elizabeth always enjoyed once she arrived safely and settled in for most of the summer.

But she was not only afraid of the deep ruts, sudden curves, and slick roads if it had been raining. She also had to pass over a large dam at Dr. Smith's pond. He was the country doctor for that vicinity. On that section of the highway was a deep curve on the bridge. She was so frightened the car might roll into the water beneath that she would hide in the foot of the backseat of their car. She even prayed softly. She'd begin worrying about the return home days before she was to leave. Just thoughts of that big dam and bad road still give her the jitters.

Thinking of bridges, the ones we crossed in that day were all wooden. They would rattle tremendously as the cars and buggies rolled over them. And they could also become slick in rainy weather. Daddy always drove very slowly over them.

I can well recall much of the two-lane highway paving that took place around the state. Now we see even small county roads paved, thank goodness. My parents lived to see four-lane highways, but I think that they would be amazed at our interstates of this period. They are certainly a far cry from what was endured for those journeys by automobiles a long time ago. The following recipes might well have been prepared after one of these tiring trips.

Bacon Omelet

1/2 cup of cooked, diced bacon
1 cup mashed potatoes
2 tablespoon milk or cream
1/2 teaspoon salt
1/8 teaspoon pepper
1 teaspoon baking powder
4 well beaten egg yolks
4 stiffly beaten egg whites
Extra fried bacon strips and parsley for garnish.

Fry bacon in heavy skillet. Remove, drain and pour off excess fat. Break into pieces and reserve. Combine potatoes, milk, seasonings, baking powder and egg yolks. Carefully fold in egg whites. Pour into hot skillet and sprinkle bacon over top. Cook over low heat until puffed brown. Fold over and garnish with extra strips of fried bacon and parsley, if desired. Serves 4.

Boiled Salad Dressing

2 tablespoons butter
1 level tablespoon flour
2 teaspoons sugar
2 eggs
1 teaspoon dry mustard
2/3 teaspoon salt
1 teaspoon pepper
1 cup vinegar

Put butter, flour, sugar, eggs, mustard, salt and pepper into the top of a double boiler. Cook over hot water until mixture begins to thicken. Add vinegar and continue cooking 3 minutes. Beat mixture occasionally while cooking. Keep in a cool, dark place. This dressing will remain good several weeks under refrigeration. It is delicious on cole slaw.

Playing paper dolls was a constant pleasure for the girls when we were growing up. This fun was never confined to a season, but was an all-year, number one enjoyment. We played with them until we were big girls, and it provided endless joy.

We preferred paper dolls that were cut out of fashion books and we had whole families of dolls, running from infants to old people, men and women, boys and girls. That was necessary because games we developed required whole families.

It took us hours to pick out the ones we wanted, then we carefully cut them from the magazines and stored them in a particular periodical, which had enough pages to accommodate our wide range of "people." Little babies were filed separately from older ones, as were other children and the grown-ups. The Sears Roebuck catalog yielded quantities of all generations. Of course Leila and I shared the various choices.

We called them "papes" for short. Often, a friend would phone and invite us over to spend the day and bring our collection with us. They traveled with care and ease, in magazines that held them in well-filed order. A game might well go on for an entire day or even be continued for several more. It was especially fun to have this simple entertainment on rainy days or in house confinement.

My sister has always had a vivid imagination, and her "papes" would become involved in the most intriguing situations. She was quite sought-after as a playing partner, to my dismay. However Martha, my inseparable friend, was most often available to play with me, and I would use some of my sister's ideas when playing with her.

Any of these games would spread out all over an entire floor. As the play developed, some of our "people" would go off on trips, visit friends, be attending school or church. It varied constantly, as our imaginations placed them in a variety of antics. Their homestead was always maintained, with some of the family still there, though the principal characters might be at the shore, in the hospital or at a party. It depended on what sort of ideas occurred to us.

Picking up after our play was an awesome undertaking. First we'd collect all of the dolls and return them to their proper pages in the magazine selected to contain them. Then the furniture had to be unfolded and made flat, to be inserted in another section of our periodical. Remember, this game might have involved the entire floor and have moved up onto the piano stool, tables or whatever had been needed for the play. We were never allowed to leave a single one unattended, and consequently were well aware of the picking up that concluded a day's play.

Of all the women's fashion magazines to which we had access, the most-treasured was the old *Delineater* periodical. The women and little girls had curly hair and baby-doll faces. I've not heard of that particular fashion book for ages and trust that it is no longer in print. Neither Mama nor Grandmother Davenport subscribed to it, much to our dismay. However, our next door neighbor, whom we called Aunt Lily, often purchased one and Leila and I were elated when she passed her copies on to us. We would pick and choose the beauties that most pleased us, and they became the prominent people in our games, because of their lovely faces. Most of these were women or older teen-agers, though a few were little girls. They were highly cherished and more rare than the ones from *Vogue* and other, more prominent periodicals.

Books of paper dolls, with separate dresses, were often presented to us as gifts. We liked them, too, but we really preferred the ones we made ourselves from magazines. The books of dolls always featured one or two little girls in their underwear, with dresses printed individually for each. The clothes were cut out, too, and could be fit over the doll by folding little attached flaps over shoulders and around arms. These were fun for some games, and we liked to make clothes for them ourselves. We'd draw a little dress, remember to add the flaps for keeping it on the girl, and usually colored them with crayons.

I wonder whatever happened to my huge books of these carefully cut-out treasures. I think Leila most probably gave hers to me when she became too old to play with them. Bet it would be as good as hitting the lottery if they could be discovered!

I hope this is still a pleasure for little girls. Playing paper dolls is such innocent joy and can occupy so much time. Having five grandsons and not one granddaughter, I don't know what young female choices are today. My own daughters played with "papes" some, but never as intensely as the girls in my youth. They were an absolute must and a complete pleasure to all of us.

Hope the following recipes will be useful for interested cooks:

Mama's shrimp creole

Sauce:
2 tablespoons chopped celery
4 tablespoons chopped onion
2 tablespoons chopped green pepper
4 tablespoons butter

Remainder of ingredients:
3 pounds raw shrimp
2 tablespoons chopped pimento
2 tablespoons tomato paste
1 teaspoon paprika
5 tablespoons flour
1 cup meat stock or canned broth
1 1/2 cups sour cream
3 tablespoons cream
1/2 pound sliced fresh mushrooms or equivalent in cans
3 tablespoons white wine

Make sauce of first four ingredients. Cook slowly in butter until vegetables are tender. Blend flour gently into the meat stock to avoid lumps. When mixture begins to thicken, add remaining ingredients and sauce continue to cook, stirring constantly to avoid lumps. Add the cleaned and deveined shrimp, which should total about 1 1/2 to 2 pounds once dressed. Continue cooking for about 3 to 5 minutes. Just before serving, add wine. Serve over steamed rice. Makes 4 to 6 servings.

Lemon chess pie

1 stick butter
2 cups sugar
1 1/2 tablespoons cornmeal
1 tablespoon flour
5 eggs
Juice and grated rinds of 2 large lemons
2 unbaked 8-inch pie shells

Cream butter and sugar. Add eggs one at a time. Blend in flour and meal. Add juice and rinds of lemons. Mix well. Pour into unbaked pie shells. Cook at 425 degrees for 10 minutes. Reduce oven to 325 degrees and continue baking for 10 to 15 additional minutes, or until pie filling doesn't "jiggle" when pie is moved. Center must be firm and slightly brown on top. These pies can be served warm or cold and they freeze well. They do not have to be refrigerated overnight, but refrigeration is recommended after 24 hours.

One of the things that most excited our own little Hooks family each spring was going to the woods for wildflowers.

We'd drive out to Daddy's farm, stop at the edge of a forest and walk inland to find our treasures, some of which Daddy would have spotted for us before our annual trek. We always followed him, who would remind us to look where we were stepping because poisonous snakes were out. We rarely made a trip without killing at least one rattler or moccasin, but it never spoiled the journey for any of us.

In those days, girls did not wear long pants of any sort. When we were going on these trips, Mama would put Leila and me into long-sleeve dresses or blouses and skirts with high-top socks or stockings that came up above our knees and under our skirts. This was supposed to be protective against briers, insects, and poison ivy.

Among the wonderful flowers we would find were large, bird's-foot violets, usually in such big beds that we could pick a handful without moving from a single spot. Then there were honeysuckles, which are really wild azaleas. These came in two colors flame and very light pink. They were handsome and always a special prize to locate, with their nice, light fragrance. Leila and I liked the pink ones better, but our parents thought the deep orangish ones were more beautiful.

And, of course, there were dogwoods in abundance, as well as crabapple blooms and sweet shrubs. The tiny brown flowers of the latter we picked off the bushes and tied in the corner of our handkerchiefs so that, when slightly crushed, they emitted a delightful fragrance. Sometimes we put a few in a little box to carry back home for sharing at school.

One day we came upon a large slope covered with bluefly iris. Though the stems on these blossoms were extremely short, Mama wanted some for low vases. I also remember grancy gray-beard bushes, which we never picked. We greatly admired the trailing, long, fringelike white blossoms that resembled a soft beard, but the flower's stems were thick, and we had been told they would die before we could get them home. My parents also were careful about preserving these wild beauties for future years.

Rain lilies were found in abundance in swampy places. A wagon load of these delicate flowers, along with smilax, had been brought to our Davenport grandparents' home for Mama and Daddy's wedding. Since they were married on April 17, 1912, I believe the timing of this column must be correct for the lilies' blooming season. In order to use the blooms properly, a large white sheet had been attached to the wall before which the vows were to be spoken. The vines and lilies were gracefully fastened to the sheet, completely covering it. It certainly must have made a perfect background for that special event, which foretold their more than fifty years together.

On our journeys, we all carried buckets, large ones for parents and smaller ones for children. We filled them from a stream that ran through the woods before placing our treasures into them, short-stemmed blossoms in the little containers and longer branches in the big ones. We generally left our pails near the stream and returned to them when our hands were full. Before we carried them back to the car, we'd pour out most of the water so they would be light enough for us to carry, though there was always enough moisture left across the bottoms to keep the pickings fresh on our journey home. Just before we left, Mama would sprinkle the tops with fresh spring water. Near the stream, several kinds of wild ferns grew. Mama would sometimes try to uproot a few of these for potting. Once they had found their way to a very shady place on our front porch, they had to be watered often.

If we had chosen a Sunday for this expedition, the sisters had some blossoms that were fresh enough to take to our teachers at school the next day. We always shared with special neighbors and grandparents, which was almost as much fun as the hunting and picking.

Flowers of all varieties bring such joy that it is pleasant just to think and write about them. But I must say, I consider our wildflower hunting unique and a true delight.

Here are some very old-fashioned recipes I hope will be of interest or use to you.

Aunt Cloe's muffins

1 quart sifted plain flour
1 1/2 pints buttermilk
1 teaspoon baking soda
1 teaspoon salt
2 tablespoons corn meal
2 eggs, well-beaten
1 tablespoon sugar

Beat the eggs and add the sugar and milk. Sift flour, with soda, salt and meal. Add to the liquid and beat 1 minute. Bake at 400 degrees in muffin tins that have been greased and filled to 3/4 full. Bake until lightly brown, about 10 to 12 minutes. This batter may also be cooked on top of the stove by dropping in dollops on top of a hot skillet. Flip over when the bottoms are brown.

Corn fritters

1 tea cup milk
3 eggs, separated
1 pint of green corn, grated
Salt to taste
Enough flour to form a batter
Lard for frying

Separate eggs and beat yolks very lightly; to the yolks add corn, milk, salt and flour, to form a batter. Beat very hard, then stir in the stiffly beaten egg whites. Drop batter, a spoonful at the time, on a very hot skillet with just enough lard for covering the bottoms. Turn, brown on the reverse side. Drain.

I remember a little mischief that my dearest friend, Martha, and I got into when we were about eight. We still laugh about our prank as though it were just yesterday. It happened on an afternoon in the early spring. We had climbed to the top of the roof of a chicken house in her back yard to make a playhouse up there. We had begun moving utensils to make our mud pies along with a box to be used as a table.

Suddenly and almost simultaneously we spotted a row of late-blooming, yellow-centered narcissuses. They were in the very back of the yard belonging to Miss Miriah Harrold.

The two of us decided that it would be just great to jump off the end of the chicken house roof into the neighbor's yard. We could quickly pick a bountiful bouquet of those blooms for our mothers. We knew that Miss Miriah would never see us. After all, she was so old she walked with a gold-handled cane and even had a live-in female companion to take care of her. For no reason, except that she kept to herself, we thought that she was cross and we were jealous that she had such gorgeous, sweet-smelling flowers.

In no time at all, we had picked about as many of these fragrant blooms as our small hands could hold. Now the problem for us was to return to Martha's yard, over the fence, without hurting the flowers . We decided our best chance was to poke the blossoms through the wide squares of the wires in the partition separating the property. This was accomplished at the lowest part of the wall. Now our hands were free to climb back into the original yard, retrieve the flowers and give them to our mothers.

As we gathered them into our hands again and began our trek to each house we realized that the first question presented to us would be, "Where did you get such lovely blossoms?" Stuck and struck with this realization, we stood for a few minutes before deciding on a plan.

We agreed that it might be best to just take them to old, cross Miss Miriah. After all, they really were hers and we had actually stolen them.

Down to the corner we walked and up to her house. We gently, and almost frighteningly, rang the door bell. It was promptly answered by her companion, who expressed delight at the sight of the flowers in the hands of two rather dirty little girls.

To our horror we were invited in to hand them to the mean, old lady. But with great surprise she almost got out of the rocker at the sight of the bearers. We had no idea that she could move with such agility.

"What gorgeous bouquets you children have brought to me," she said. "I can't thank you enough. I once had some similar to those growing far back in my yard (here we cringed with horror) but I am so old now I can't get way out there. I doubt that they are still blooming."

Then she asked her companion to make a little tea for all of us, and to be sure and bring out some cookies. She also was instructed to take us to the nearby washroom to clean our hands. We were so stunned that the constant giggles we usually emitted were gone. In that little bathroom we were astonished at the dainty soaps and sparkling, white, linen towels. We scrubbed hard in order to avoid staining the towels. We also had a quiet chance to whisper about what had developed.

When we returned to the living room, we found our hostess to be a dear and most pleasant person. She asked about our parents and even my grandparents, whom she knew quite well. We also told her about our schoolwork. By that time Miss Davenport returned. She carried a large silver tray. It held a silver teapot, four dainty cups and saucers, silver spoons, a cream pitcher and bowl with lumps of sugar. There were cinnamon-coated tea cakes on a china plate in addition.

The beverage was poured and we were urged to add several lumps of the sugar to it as well as some of the thick cream. There were adorable, tiny silver tongs for removing the cubes of sugar. Linen napkins were passed as well as the cookies, and we became more relaxed and pleased with the way our flower picking had evolved.

When our little party ended, our hostess urged us to come back to see her, saying that she got very lonely. Miss Davenport seemed equally enthusiastic about a return call. We vowed that we would, and I'm sure we must have done so, but the later visits were not as startling or memorable as the first.

The good lesson that came from all of this was evident. We now knew that we should return a person's property and also not misjudge people simply because they were old and not often seen. From that day on, Martha and I would tell any of our friends that Miss Miriah was not a cross, old person, just lonely.

I wish I had her cookie recipe to offer to you but it was not given to me. Instead I will supply you with some others from our little town of Americus. These might also be as old as Miss Miriah. I well remember enjoying these treats when I was growing up in Americus.

Jellied Ham Salad

1 envelope plain gelatin
1/4 cupful of cold water
1 cupful boiling chicken stock
1 cupful of chopped ham
About 1/2 teaspoon cayenne
Lemon juice to taste
1 cup heavy cream, whipped

Soak gelatin in water and add boiling broth. Stir well to dissolve and strain. Add the ham, which should be highly seasoned with cayenne, and lemon juice. Let stand until mixture begins to thicken, then fold in the cream whipped to a stiff froth. Turn into a wetted mold. When firm, turn out on a bed of lettuce leaves and garnish with mayonnaise.

Tea-Bread Muffins

1 tablespoon butter
3 tablespoons sugar, or to taste
2 eggs, separated
2 cups flour
1 cup milk
2 heaping teaspoons baking powder
Pinch of salt

Mix sugar, butter and egg yolks together and beat well. Add flour, baking powder and salt, alternating with milk. Fold in stiffly beaten egg whites. Pour into greased muffin pans and bake at 400 degrees for about 10 minutes or until lightly brown on tops. Serve hot with sweet butter or jam.

Good manners were very important among the families where I grew up and especially in my own. Children were instructed at an early age to be obedient and also to follow the rules set by their parents. This was not just a "please" and "thank you" lesson. It was much more serious and involved.

Never would one of us have called an adult by a first name. It was always "Miss Ruby" or "Mr. Walter" when the older friends were close with our families. Otherwise we called them Mr. and Mrs. Often. If a person was very close and dear to us, we might have called them "Aunt Mattie" and "Uncle Tom." But it was entirely irregular for us to address our elders in any other way than the above.

I remember very early in my life being told that I should rise to my feet, if seated, when an adult entered the room. It was also customary to offer my chair to the visitor.

One incident I'll never forget was the day I was rocking my baby doll in the little white rocker I had received for Christmas. "Aunt" Lily, our next-door neighbor, whom I adored, came into the room to see us and I hopped out of my seat quickly to provide her a chair. Everybody burst into laughter, which distressed me greatly for I thought that I had done something very improper. Consequently I broke into tears thinking that I had been at great fault.

Mama quickly came to the rescue, realizing my dilemma, grabbed me up in her arms and explained that the laughter had come because my chair was too small for our guest. I was assured that I had been proper and "Aunt" Lily even tried to sit in my white rocker just to further explain the circumstances. Of course, this was funny to all of us and I shall always appreciate the fact that she was such a good sport and eager to help out a sensitive child.

From an early age, boys were taught that they were to remove their hats indoors. As they grew older they were taught to tip their hats, as their fathers did, to ladies when they passed them on the streets. It disturbs me

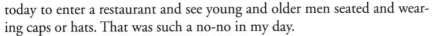

today to enter a restaurant and see young and older men seated and wearing caps or hats. That was such a no-no in my day.

My maternal grandfather, Fred Davenport, was a stately man who walked to and from work twice daily to his office as postmaster in Americus. He held this job for thirty years. Grandfather walked with long strides and always carried a cane, not for necessity, but more for looks. One day, as he approached a fruit stand close to his place of work, he saw two women coming from the market. He promptly removed his hat, in gentlemanly fashion, and at the same time his right foot slid on a banana peel. Consequently, he hit the ground on that knee and it appeared as though he had bowed to the ladies with hat removed. He laughingly told us about it and said that he could see the women turning back to look at him several times as they walked away. Surely they felt that he had outdone himself with his greeting for them.

The gentlemanly manners for young boys included the rule to always pull out the chair for a lady when being seated at the table for a meal. They were also to open car doors for females and help them into the vehicle. Of course, their fathers set the example for them.

When we had family dinners I remember how furious it made my cousin, the late George Hooks, to have to seat me properly at these events. We were exactly the same age, probably had been playing marbles, jack straws or climbing trees together prior to the call for enjoying our meal together. Then *WHY* should he have to be so courteous to his same-age cousin just because I was a girl? But manners were manners and it was required of him. This gentle behavior was most important in my era. Children learned these graces early and most never forgot that training.

Toothpicks were another manners issue. My parents abhorred them. We rarely ate out, but when we did it was tempting to pick up one of the little objects for our use. Mama always reminded us that they should never be used in public. "You wouldn't brush your teeth walking down the street, now would you?" she said. I continue to have the same feeling about these objects.

Obedience was also foremost in our earliest training. If we disobeyed, we could be punished. The rod was not used, but switches certainly were.

I remember that my parents kept a peach-tree cutting very visible on the mantel in our family room. It was seldom used because they found that my sister and I wanted very much to always please them and consequently were obedient. They would often say, "I don't want to use that switch on you so be careful how you speak to me or obey," as the case might have been.

If either of us, my sister or I, had been fresh, sassy or naughty we would have been corrected promptly, possibly with the switch. The truth was we so adored our gentle parents that we could easily be shamed into prompt behavior. I cried desperately if I felt that I had displeased either of them in any way. Leila was more adventurous and had several tappings on her legs with the peach-tree whip. This made it quite evident to both of us that the constant reminder on the mantel was readily available when needed.

I must add, however, that neither my sister nor I were ever abused. We readily knew, if punishment occurred, that we had asked for it and were satisfied that we were still dearly loved in our home. We were more fortunate than many children today who are not as close to their loving parents.

Following are several recipes that I found in a little Rumford Baking Powder cookbook that Mother had. Recipes were not readily available in printed form in her day as they are now, but could be ordered from companies like the one above. Once received, women traded the new recipes with neighbors and friends.

Coffee Layer Cake

1/2 cup butter
1 cup brown sugar
2 eggs
1/2 cup molasses
1/2 cup cold coffee
2 cups flour
1/2 teaspoon mixed spices of your choice
1/2 teaspoon salt
3 teaspoons baking powder

Beat butter and sugar until creamy; add eggs, then the molasses and coffee. Lastly add flour, salt, spices and baking powder, sifted together. Bake in layers at 350 degrees about 20 minutes. Put together with frosting of your choice or serve plain. Delicious cut while hot and served with fresh butter.

Cheese Puffs

2 well beaten eggs
3/4 cup flour
3/4 cup milk
1 teaspoon baking powder
Salt and pepper to taste
1/2 to 3/4 cup sharp, grated cheese
Fat for frying

Beat eggs well and add to milk. Sift together the flour, baking powder and seasonings. Add cheese and mix to a stiff batter with the milk and eggs. Beat well and drop by spoonful into hot, deep fat. Cook until golden brown. Drain and serve hot.

One Woman's Garbage Becomes Children's Treasure

It was a late May afternoon, shortly before school was to close for the summer. Our little Harrold Avenue crowd in Americus was walking home from classes, more or less together. As we rounded the corner of our street we saw a huge pile of assorted trash. It had been dumped on the road beside the house of our neighbor, "Miss" Aleen, a rather affluent person who discarded quantities. Eyes grew big at what we observed in the bounty, and a quick decision was made by our group.

All of this garbage seemed more like loot to us, and we stopped only long enough to glance at what we might find useful. Every child went home to put down our books, gather large paper bags and return to the pile. Some of the boys who had wagons pulled them back to the treasure heap. All of us were running for fear we would miss out on what we most wanted.

I remember going for the pattern books to be used for paper dolls. I also found an ostrich feather, some cloth scraps, buttons, old compacts with the mirrors intact, and sheet music. We had a piano at our house and Mother played well, so I felt the new pieces were a real prize.

My friend, Martha, and I shared many of our prizes since we played so constantly together our loot could be interchangeable. Leila was in high school by this time and didn't get in on the pickings. When she returned home, she was amused to hear about our treasures and how we had gotten them. She made me feel very proud that I had made so many wise selections.

The boys eagerly looked for nails, bolts, and screws and one even found a wheel. He didn't know just how he might use it, but knew it would be handy for something. They also grabbed for heavy cords, old lamps and some broken metal objects. Their interests were not those of the girls, so I only vaguely remember a few of their choices.

There must have been about twelve of us rummaging through those attic discards. We would pick out our treasures, fill bags, return home for more empty holders, and return to the scene. On my second trip Mother supplied me with a peach basket to use and I shared it with my friend. As the pile went down, we began to find high-heeled shoes, old hats, scarves, pocketbooks, and costume jewelry. This was all perfect for the girls to play dress-up.

Children in my era did not have shoes with heels made to fit them. Long gowns and ornaments like those available today were not heard of in our time. Today they can play dress-up in "store-bought" sizes to fit, but we had to rely on hand-me-downs for our games. We didn't mind one bit wobbling around in discarded heels and wearing old hats and long dresses. It was fun, and we felt really grown up.

I can remember Mother and "Aunt" Mattie, sitting on our porch, which was closest to the garbage scene, rocking in chairs and laughing at our delightful project. We were all on foot and must have made many trips back and forth. Eventually the pile was reduced to almost nothing, and Mama called "Miss" Aleen to be sure that she knew the trash had been carefully removed. She also informed her that it was treated as treasures in almost every neighboring home.

Mother told me later that it tickled the provider to pieces when she informed her about the grabbing and hauling of the children. "Why, I had called a dray and driver to remove it early in the morning," she said. "I didn't want to clutter up the street with my attic discards."

Now all she had to do was have her house maid sweep up the leftovers and put them in the garbage can. It saved her great expense and certainly pleased most of the neighborhood children. It had truly been a great day for the youngsters.

For days following we sorted our treasures and put them to use. Doll clothes were made from some of the scraps at the girls' homes, and dress-up games were very prominent. Hours were spent cutting out new paper dolls and filing them in our books. Of course, we played with them too, but they first had to be sorted and taken from the magazines.

We must have been a grubby bunch when we returned home from our pillaging that warm, spring day. I can recall being scrubbed clean and even washing off some of my choices with soap and water before being allowed to use them. But what great pleasure the whole neighborhood had over a pile of junk.

All of this took place several years after World War I had ended. I know specifically because of one of the discarded pieces of piano music that I found. Mama and Daddy remembered that it had been popular during that time. Mother played it on the piano for us, and many of our friends joined in singing it.

The tune was a simple one and the lyrics funny. As I best remember the words are as follows. I don't remember the title of the song but here is what I believe we sang quite often.

"Goodbye Maw, Goodbye Paw,
Goodbye mule with the old hee haw.
I may not know what the war's about
But I'll bet, by gosh, I'll soon find out.
And oh! my sweetheart don't you fear
I'll bring you a queen for a souvenir.
I'll get you a king and a kaiser too
And that's about all one 'fella can do."

Today's recipes are more from the 1922 baking powder book mentioned earlier. It's full of dishes that I recall enjoying while growing up and I feel elated that I have come across this great find. It's about as good as sorting through attic treasures.

Chicken Souffle

2 level tablespoons butter
2 level tablespoons flour
1 1/2 cups milk or milk with chicken stock
1/2 level teaspoon salt
1/2 level teaspoon pepper
1/4 teaspoon grated lemon rind
1 cup minced chicken
3 eggs, separated
1/2 cup stale bread crumbs

Blend butter and flour in a saucepan without browning; add milk and stir until boiling. Put in the salt, pepper, bread crumbs and lemon rind. Cool and then stir in the chicken; beat egg yolks until thick and beat whites until stiff and dry. Add the beaten yolks to the chicken mixture. Fold in whites last.

Bake in a well-greased pan at 300 degrees for about 30 minutes, or until mixture becomes dry on top and is lightly brown. Serve at once.

Horseradish Dressing

1 cup heavy cream
1 level teaspoon grated fresh or dehydrated horseradish
2 tablespoons lemon juice
Salt and paprika to taste

Beat the cream until quite thick. Add horseradish. If dehydrated horse-radish is used, pour over it a tablespoon of cold water and allow water to be absorbed before adding to cream. Put in lemon juice slowly, stirring all the time; season to taste and serve very cold. Delicious on fresh tomatoes, with roast beef and baked fish.

Warm Nights On Sleeping Porch

It was about the end of Spring that excitement zoomed in the Glenn Hooks household in Americus. The weather in our area was now warm enough to move our family of four out to the sleeping porch for our night's rest. The fresh air in this screened in room was considered both healthy and extremely refreshing on the warm nights that had begun. The really hot evenings lay ahead.

The porch would have been scrubbed from bottom to top since it had idled for many months. The beds used in there also were washed, the mattresses aired and it was great to know that such a popular room in our little house would soon be in use. It still holds many delightful memories for me.

As the youngest member of my family I was usually the first to awaken. The sleeping porch offered many advantages for such an early riser. I had been carefully trained not to awaken the other sleepers and consequently had to quietly entertain myself until the others arose.

Lying in my bed gave a wide expanse of vision and many wonderful opportunities to quietly amuse myself. The view was so broad that I could easily see cloud formations. I could picture them as faces, animals, mountains—just name it. It was a delight to watch them change into another object as they moved. Children's imaginations seem endless, when given the opportunity, and I'm glad to have had one.

There were two trees close to the sleeping porch that offered their shade for this room. One was a large mulberry, with tremendous leaves. The other was a pecan with many branches. I loved to watch them move and sway with the breeze. However, their best advantage for my early morning entertainment was to watch the birds fly in and out between their leaves.

These lovely feathered creatures particularly enjoyed the ripened mulberries that seemed constant throughout our summer. They would fly in after special tempting choices. Sometimes two would fight over a particularly luscious one. That brought loud chirping and seemed funny.

Quite often the birds would eat so greedily that they would become drunk from the juice and fly around in weird swirls. Occasionally they would even bump into the screens of our porch. This would awaken other members of the family, and we all thought it was so entertaining that we'd lie there and watch their antics together for a brief time.

As soon as all arose, we went into the main part of the house for breakfast. I could tell them that I had seen bluejays and cardinals, two that I knew distinctly, along with small sparrows. I recall spotting a small, yellowish bird, and was excited to tell about it.

"Probably a wild canary," my father said. That proved a satisfactory answer for me then, but I often now wonder just what it might have been.

During stormy weather we could easily watch the rain falling from our great vantage point on that porch. When there was lightning and loud thunder, my sister and I were at first frightened. But Daddy taught us to watch the brightness glow between the trees and clouds. Then he instructed us to measure our pulse and start counting as soon as we saw a streak.

"The number you've reached when you hear the thunder means that the bolt is that many miles away," he said.

That both waylaid our fears and gave us something to concentrate on. If the rain began to blow through the screens, my father was quick to jump out of bed and lower the heavy canvas curtains over the openings. They were ordinarily rolled up high in order to catch as much fresh air as possible. But it was fun to see them come tumbling down and hear the drops beat against them.

Summer nights brought new things for me to enjoy. I was put to bed earlier than the rest of the family since I was the youngest. Before falling asleep I often listened for certain sounds. I could hear nearby trains, their bells clanging and their chugging and slowing to a steaming stop. This would evoke wonders of where they might be going and who could possibly be on them, traveling to where? I also was able to identify a neighbor's dog's bark or hear a car coming down our street. On evenings of a bright, full moon, roosters in nearby yards would crow. This was a unique treat.

In our town almost everybody that I knew had a sleeping porch. Apparently our entire village felt that sleeping porches were essential. They were never fancy but were functional. Ours was added on to the back of the original house. All of these summer rooms were built with wide openings to invite in as much cool night air as possible. Ours did not have glass windows attached, as many people's did. I'm glad for I truly loved those canvas curtains that protected us against bad rains. I can envision them tumbling down right now.

These memories are before the time of air-conditioned homes or even large box fans. Our little sleeping porch was cool and most comfortable and answered the problem of heat well. I consider myself very fortunate to have enjoyed so many advantages offered to me by this now outdated arrangement for summer sleeping. And I shall always treasure the memories.

Here is a healthy cookie recipe that Mama often made for us.

Applesauce-Bran Cookies

1 2/3 cups sifted all-purpose flour
1 teaspoon baking soda
1/4 teaspoon each: nutmeg, ground cloves, allspice and salt
1/2 cup low-fat margarine
4 tablespoons sugar
1 egg
1 cup unsweetened applesauce
1/3 cup golden raisins
1 cup 40% Bran Flakes cereal

Preheat oven to 375 degrees. Sift dry ingredients into medium-size bowl. In separate bowl, beat margarine, sugar and egg until light and fluffy. Alternate dry ingredients and applesauce, mixing well after each addition. Stir in raisins and cereal, blend gently. Drop by rounded teaspoons onto cookie sheets that have been sprayed with nonstick vegetable spray. Bake 15 minutes or until golden brown. Makes 3 dozen 3 1/2-inch cookies. Remove from pans as they come from oven and cool on racks before storing. Recipe can be doubled easily, or smaller size cookies made. Freeze well.

During May we would always drive out to Daddy's farm. This time we were in search of a real treat that our entire family enjoyed. There were mayhaw trees or bushes in the swampy part of the woods where we previously had visited to gather wild flowers.

We females were once again dressed in long-sleeved shirts, high knit stockings and tight-fitting skirts. As before, this protected us from insects, poison ivy and scratches from briers. The ride out would be hot, in our complete-covering attire. But once we were in the shade of the forest, welcome breezes cooled us.

Mother, Leila, and I knew from past experiences that we needed to walk quite a distance inland to find our treasures. Daddy would have spotted the ripened fruit for us before our annual trek.

He would remind us to look where we were stepping because poisonous snakes were out from their winter hibernation. We rarely made a trip without killing at least one or two rattlers or perhaps a water moccasin. The latter were especially prevalent in the swampy area where our treat awaited.

However, the search for snakes never spoiled the journey for any of us. We knew how to step wide over fallen logs in order to avoid encountering one. Also, our father had trained us to look out for areas where they might be. We had been taught that a rattler will hold its ground even in coil, so we backed off if we came near one.

Moccasins were more threatening, because we'd been told that they will chase their prey. We were always most cautious and terrified until we reached our goal unharmed. I am still in horror of these creatures.

Daddy was quick at killing snakes. He said that once they were smacked hard on their long back it would be broken. This caused them to be motionless and their heads could be crushed with whatever instrument he always took along for precaution.

We'd also been taught to make great stomping noise and yell loudly. "The snakes are just as frightened about you as we are of them," Daddy would explain. Our yelling helped clear the paths. Along with precaution, we journeyed with tremendous loudness.

When we were going to the swampy part of the woods to gather may-haws, buckets, sheets and a large galvanized tub were carried along. When we reached the trees laden with small, orange-colored fruit, the sheets would be stretched under several of the small branches and the tub placed in the center. Daddy would shake the little tree very hard and the small, ripe haws would fall into the tub with nice plunking sounds. Any that missed the mark were found on the sheets and we'd quickly pick them up and place the delicacies in our buckets. We even picked some off low limbs.

This procedure continued until we had as many as either the trees provided or Mother wanted for making jelly. Then all of our equipment would be gathered together and there was time for some woodsy fun.

Because our father had grown up on the old family farm, he knew many delightful tricks to treat my sister and me. Sometimes he would cut the top off a small pine tree and instruct us to sit on it. He would pull the end of the trunk a short distance until the weight of our bodies easily made it slide quickly over dry pine straw and downward to the bottom of a hill. "Do it again!" we'd scream.

His patience seemed endless, and Mama seemed to thoroughly enjoy watching our fun. If it was warm enough on that particular day, we were allowed to take off our shoes and stockings and wade in the nearby stream. Towels always were carried along for drying us off after a dip.

While we played in this manner, Daddy would hunt for small twigs or little branches. These he made into what was called a "flutter mill." It somewhat resembled a little windmill, but I've no idea in the world how it was constructed. But it was something that he had learned to make as a boy. I remember that he always carried a long pin or thin nail in his pocket to place the wheel part onto its pole when he anticipated making one of these for us.

The object would be placed at a swift area of the stream in order for the current to make it turn or "flutter." Often my sister and I would make a little dam in the water to increase the swiftness of its flow. We'd move

large rocks, small branches or anything that would help our construction. Mama would help us find necessities while the toy was being made.

Now, if any of you have never tasted the tart jelly made from mayhaws, then you have missed one of south Georgia's finest treats. It is available in gift shops locally. But our mother and grandmother made their own, as do many of my friends and relatives who still have access to them in or near Americus.

I can remember the thorough washing and pressing of the fruit that we had gathered. It would be placed aside until the next day or until the time when these wonderful women would work with it. Once it had been crushed sufficiently, it was poured into mesh bags and hung over tubs to drip overnight. Squeezings would take place periodically to extract as much juice as possible.

Once the liquid had reached a sufficient amount, the jelly - making took place. It always smelled delicious while cooking. When it was poured up and sealed into little jars we marveled at the clear, bright deep peach color that it displayed. There is no other confection that compares to it in my opinion. Perhaps a lot of my feeling is also bundled up in the recollection of gathering the fruit as well as watching the preparation of the end result.

I am giving you the recipe for this treat, should you be lucky enough to perhaps find some mayhaws at a roadside market. Put a big spoonful of this jelly on a hot, buttered biscuit and you've got it made. I've also included an additional recipe that seems a little different and a nice late spring treat.

Mayhaw Jelly

Juice of fruit
3/4 cup sugar to each cup of juice
Spice

Wash and drain berries. Place in large vessel with water to cover. When this begins to boil mash berries at intervals until they are all mashed and tender. Then strain through a colander lined with a cloth. Place the juice into a large vessel. Bring juice to a boil. Add 3/4 cup sugar to each cup of juice and cook until it drops from spoon in a thick sheet. This is worth all the trouble it takes.

Cheese and Pimento Salad

4 (3-ounce) blocks cream cheese
1 (4-ounce) jar pimientos
Mayonnaise
Lettuce leaves

Break up cream cheese, at room temperature, and mash with a fork until creamy. Grind the pimientos through the fine blade of the meat chopper and mix thoroughly with the cheese, adding a very little of the juice from the pimento jar. Beat until a light and fluffy mass forms. Heap on lettuce leaves and surround with mayonnaise dressing. It is also most delicious and pretty.

Summer

"No more lessons, no more books, no more teacher's sassy looks." SCHOOL'S OUT!

This little verse followed by the great exclamation would be chanted by our Harrold Avenue crowd all the way from Furlow Grammar to our homes. I loved school and so did most of my friends, but the thought of a long vacation filled with play time and fewer cares was certainly a delight.

All of us had special joys and games during the summer months, but our entire little street liked the free evenings when we could play outdoors until bed time. Ages made no difference for those wonderful nighttime games. The very little ones sat on their porches with parents and delighted in watching the activities of their older siblings or friends. I had been in that position and remember it well.

The unpaved street meant we could draw lines and circles in the earth for various games. There was a large, bright street light in the center of our block that created sufficient glow for us to see well. All parents turned on their front porch lights to add to the illumination.

The evening games enjoyed were different than daytime ones. That was mainly because they involved all of us. During the mornings and afternoons we had chores or played with just a few friends. But those night "play outs" included all.

We played "Snake in the Gulley" where drawn parallel lines across the road would form the imaginary ravine where "the snake" ran his course. We counted out for the person to be "it" and that one became the serpent. Teams were divided on each side of the entrenchment, and we would run back and forth across the lines trying not to be caught.

"Bum, Bum, Bum," is still a well known favorite. It was kind of a charade. Two sides were appointed, and each would work up a pantomime to be guessed by the other team. As we began to present our decision, a team would approach the other saying, "Bum, bum, bum here we come" and the other would respond with "What's your trade?" Response, "Sweet lemonade," then the latter would say, "Show us some." At this point the first group would give two or three initials representing the activity being shown. This was a hint about the acting. Once the second group guessed the subject, they would repeat the procedure producing their plan.

For the life of me I can't remember how we played "Prison Base," but it was a sort of hiding play. A place for the jail was chosen and once a person was caught, probably from a hidden place, they were put into the drawn off area designed for the convicted. I mostly remember the name and a prison.

My favorite, by far, was just plain hide and go seek. Our group designated a small area close to the street light with about three houses and yards on each side. We could not go out of bounds at the risk of being eliminated from further play or becoming the next "it" to hunt for the hiders. Many trees and large shrubbery or fences and posts were included and made excellent places to conceal ourselves.

After counting out to determine who was to be "it," that person would put his or her head against the light post, with hands or arms over eyes, and count by fives to 100. The group would scamper to chosen spots and either catch base on our own, which freed us, or be caught. First caught was the next hunter.

All of the above is procedure, but one thing that made it more fun in my neighborhood was a little jingle that we used. While the hunter was counting out, a semi-circle would be drawn by finger on the back of the person counting out. With eyes hidden, an appointed player would take a finger and draw a half circle on the back of the counter. As this was being done the entire group would say in unison, "Draw a little semi-circle sign it with a dot." At this point, a player would administer a tap in the center of the imaginary half circle. The counting would continue unbroken until 100 had been reached.

At this point the "it" person could open eyes, turn to the crowd and try to guess who might have signed the dot. All of us would be saying, "This little finger did it!" If correct in catching the dotter, then that person traded and had to pick up where the first "it" had left off.

There's not a one of us who enjoyed these playing out games on those hot summer nights who wouldn't tell you in a minute that it was the most fun we can remember about our growing up days. There are five still living in Americus and two on that same street who inherited their parents' homes.

You will be reading about many more games that we played as a group and individually. But the playing-out nights top the list for many of us. The beauty of it all was having such a congenial neighborhood. The big children helped the smaller ones, and we all seemed to look after each other. Ages and sizes made no difference. What simple enjoyment this created that is still remembered by so many of us.

You might like to try these good family dishes.

Au Gratin Potatoes

3 cups thick sliced potatoes, peeled
1 1/2 cups grated extra sharp cheese
1 cup rich white sauce
1 teaspoon finely diced onion or juice of same
Salt and red pepper to taste

Boil potatoes until tender, but not too done. Cook for about 10 minutes. Drain. Add onion or onion juice to white sauce. In greased casserole dish put half potatoes, salt, pepper and half of the white sauce in bottom layer. Top with half of the cheese. Repeat for second layer, using all remaining ingredients with a thick topping of cheese. Bake at 400 degrees for 20 minutes or until potatoes test thoroughly done and sauce is bubbly.

Kisses With Pecans

4 egg whites
Pinch of salt
1 teaspoon cream of tartar
1 cup granulated sugar
1/2 teaspoon vanilla
1 cup coarsely chopped pecans
2 tablespoons cocoa, optional

Beat egg whites until stiff. Add salt and cream of tartar and continue beating, slowly adding sugar and vanilla. When extremely stiff, fold in pecans. Drop by teaspoonful on ungreased cookie sheets. Bake at 275 degrees for about 25 minutes or until dry and lightly brown. If cocoa is used, add along with sugar and vanilla. Makes about 50 kisses.

When I was growing up in my small town, Americus, the best days of our very hot summer weeks were when Essy came in his wagon selling hunks of ice. This was during the 1920s, and he was our ice man. In that period few people had electrically powered refrigerators. Our cold storage was called an "ice box." Large blocks of ice were placed in a special compartment of the fridge that allowed the melting ice to drip into a pan beneath the storage area. In some cases a funnel was inserted into a small hole in the floor and the liquid went straight to the ground. The equipment was generally put on screened-in back porches.

But the important thing to the children on Harrold Avenue was that Essy came to make his deliveries twice a week. Our street was unpaved and few cars traveled it, which meant that we could surround the ice-filled wagon that was pulled by Jake, a rather thin, old mule. Little did we object to the heat on ice days when that good man came.

Essy would start ringing the big cow bell that he carried, as he turned the corner of our street to announce his arrival for purchasers. The minute it was heard doors would automatically fly open on most of the houses. The children would pop out ready and happy to greet their special friend. Our mothers would join us quickly to place their orders and wait with large pans or buckets for the supply of ice.

What was so exciting about Essy's visits was to hold our hands under the block of ice as it was sawed by our strong-armed, black friend. We would catch the shavings which we called "snow" in our hot little hands and promptly eat it. The recipients could collect this treat only at their own homes. My sister and I had to share, and so did other siblings up and down the long block.

Essy was so good to all of us that even if he had a block of ice on the wagon that already was cut to specifications, he could not disappoint his young friends. He would simply shove it to the back of the wagon under a large piece of canvas that covered his supply and saw away on a new piece. One might have easily seen the delight in our faces as he cooperated so thoroughly with his "chillun." Each of us was pleased for all on our street to get their full share when he stopped at the various houses.

The entire group envied Brown Small. He was an only child and his mother had a large family whom she entertained often. She ALWAYS had a big order for Essy. And Brown got to catch a tremendous amount of snow. Sometimes he was good about sharing with special friends, but it depended on the heat of the day and how fast he could eat his supply.

We constantly were cautioned to "be careful, you must keep your hands futher away from the saw. I don't want to hurt none of my 'chillun.'" We obediently took his timely advice. After he had cut the desired size block for his customers, he would pick it up with huge tongs that gripped the chunk securely. I recall marveling at his precision for gripping with these tongs.

Since it was hot weather all of the children would be barefoot. An added advantage of Essy's visits was following the wooden, slit-floor wagon to the end of the block. We would sort of line up and walk in the trail of water from melting ice that splashed in the red clay of our unpaved street.

Sometimes, if the puddle was large at our house, Leila, my sister, and I would stand in it and stomp our feet to cool them off. We also called this making "grandpa soap." I never quite knew why we called it this, possibly because a foam would rise as we swiftly beat our feet into the soft, red clay mud. All of our friends made "soap" too, not just on ice wagon days but often following a summer shower.

I remember very distinctly one day when Essy allowed me to ring his huge bell for him. At that time in my life it was surely the equivalent of winning an Oscar in today's world! I don't recall that anybody else was ever chosen for such a distinguished honor. My sister told me it was because I was the youngest and had asked politely for the privilege. I didn't care what was the reason and still don't. It was a fine moment.

Our mothers would often allow us to give cookies to Essy, but his hands were always so wet he would ask us just to "put them on the seat of my wagon, Sugar. I'll have to eat them later. Thank you, thank you," he would say in a gentle voice. We also got permission from time to time to offer poor old Jake a lump of sugar or an apple. This, too, had to be put on the front of the wagon. Since the animal wore blinders over the sides of his eyes, we were told not to pat him for fear he might jerk and hurt one of us. Essy was always looking after the safety of his young friends. I trust, at this point in my life, that Essy might also have been afraid of losing some of his ice to the dirt street.

As fall and winter came along, Essy returned to the ice house, where we would see him and his big smile only if our father went to the plant to purchase the family's supply. My sister and I would always ask if he was there. Naturally Essy seemed pleased to be summoned. And, of course, we wanted to speak to him. He was probably our very best friend. I hope he was offered some of the following delicacies.

Peach Upside-Down Cake

Topping:
5 to 6 large, well-ripened peaches
1/2 cup brown sugar
1/3 stick butter
1/2 cup pecan halves
Cake:
1 1/4 cups plain flour
2 1/2 teaspoons baking powder
1 teaspoon salt
1 1/4 cups sugar
1/3 cup soft butter
1/3 cup milk
1 egg
1/3 cup additional milk
1 teaspoon vanilla

In a large, deep, iron skillet over low heat, melt butter and sprinkle brown sugar over top. Cook slowly to melt sugar. Peel and slice peaches from top to bottoms to form semicircles. They should be about 1/4-inch thick slices. When sugar melts, remove pan from heat and carefully place peaches in circular fashion around the skillet on top of butter and sugar mixture. Put pecan halves around to fill any crevices. Set aside.

To make cake batter, mix dry ingredients and add first 1/3 cup of milk and softened butter. Mix well, then add remaining ingredients, blending carefully. Pour batter over the topping in skillet and bake for 25 minutes at 375 degrees.

When brown on top, with some of the juices and sugar appearing at the edges of the skillet, remove from the oven. Allow to cool 10 to 15 minutes. Run a knife around the edges of the skillet and invert the cake on a plate held over the top of the pan when turning. The cake will then have a beautiful caramelized peach and nut topping. Serve with whipped heavy cream.

Grandmother Davenport's Strawberry Short Cake

2 cups strawberries, washed, sliced and sugared to taste
2 cups flour
3 teaspoons baking powder
1/2 teaspoon salt
4 level tablespoons shortening
Enough milk or water to make a soft dough
1/2 stick of butter
Whipped cream for topping

Prepare berries and set aside. Mix dough by adding dry ingredients together and cutting in shortening. Mix in liquid. Flatten dough by hands to about 1/2 -inch thick oval shapped mound. Bake at 450 degrees until lightly brown on top. Cool slightly and split entire oval down the middle. Pull out soft crumbs and reserve for future use. Butter both sides of crusty, split bread while hot. Fill bottom half with 2/3 of prepared berries. Lay second half on top, butter lightly and add remaining berries.

Serve with bountiful amount of whipped cream over top. Cut in wide slices across the oval. Makes 10 servings. (Grandmother always reserved a little strawberry juice for adding to the whipped cream making the mound appear pink when served.)

The Fourth of July was seldom celebrated with grandeur when I was growing up. People usually had family gatherings and took out picnics to nearby ponds, lakes or recreation areas. Many were on vacation and out of town during this time. Because my Grandfather Davenport was postmaster, I well recall that no mail was delivered on that date. He seldom took a vacation, so this was a treat for him.

I wrote elsewhere that the children in my part of the world shot fireworks at Christmas-time. Santa even brought ours to us, and we gathered with cousins and other relatives and fired away on my Uncle Tommy's farm. There was a field close to the house that lay dormant until planting time. That was where our combined display was fired. But never on July 4.

Perhaps friends who had big flags put them out by their houses for celebration on that day. But they were not flown all over town. It was simply another hot, summer day with time off for many workers.

I do vividly recall, with great pleasure, one big parade and celebration held on the birthday of our country during my growing-up years. This was arranged in conjunction with the unveiling of the "Doughboy Monument," a life-size statue of a World War I infantryman.

There was a big parade around the streets of downtown Americus. I remember several flag-draped cars in the procession carrying state and city dignitaries. There were even a few district congressional figures from the nation's capital represented. The high school band played and marched, and so did a big troop of Boy Scouts. A large number of World War I veterans were the main marching feature. The latter group trailed the parade in order to be ready to encircle the new monument when the unveiling took place.

Many of the veterans in the parade were close friends of my parents. Daddy had lost one of his closest buddies in the Great War, which he could not enter since he was married and my older sister, Leila, was just a baby. He had great admiration for those who fought the sad battles so brilliantly. He called out to some of his friends as they passed us while standing on the street.

I don't recall that the children had small American flags in hand as we see today. They were not as easy to come by then, and just attending the parade showed our family's backing of the community and its effort. I was a grade-school child at the time because I remember standing on the sidewalk and not being on Daddy's shoulders to see the procession.

The citizens of our community raised money for the statue that no one had yet seen. But all were eager to view the newest landmark for our town and to pay tribute to the brave soldiers of our most recent war.

My family had arrived on the scene early in order for us to have a good stand for the parade. Since the monument was to be in the center of Lee and Lamar streets right at "Grandfather's" post office we chose that general area for viewing. Following speeches about the the history and purpose of the war and recognizing many of the brave Americus veterans, as well as the ones who had been killed, the cloth was removed from the monument for grand observation on all sides.

My cousin, Quimby Melton, Jr., who lives in Griffin, has so well described this statue in his recently published book, *The History of Griffin, Ga. 1840–1940* that I shall quote him in telling about it. A similar monument was erected in his city in 1929. After much research by R.J. Petrovich, our Telegraph librarian, she has found that the sculptor was E. M. Viquesney who lived in Indiana. She also discovered that similar monuments were placed in towns and cities over the entire country about this same time.

In Melton's well-written book, he said: "The monument is a life-size image of an American fighting man in World War I. The bronze doughboy stands in a tangle of barbed wire atop a granite boulder. His mouth is open in battle cry and his right arm is raised to throw a hand grenade, which is visible in his fist. He wears wrap leggings and is moving forward. A bullet-action rifle, bayonet affixed, hangs from his left hand; its strap is loose and ready for instant use in aiming.

"A rifle belt is around his waist and a canteen is attached to it on his right hip and a first aid kit on his left one. A gas mask hangs upon his chest. He has a pack on his back with an empty bayonet scabbard attached to its left side. He wears a metal helmet called a tin hat, and its strap is beneath his chin."

The monument is so realistic that you feel as if you might speak to the soldier himself. Melton also told me that the infantrymen in that war, one in which his father had fought with distinction, were called "doughboys" because the mud through which they had to tramp in France was so thick that they felt as if they were walking in bread dough. The statue is considered accurate in every detail.

The statue still stands in Americus, but not at its original location. It is now in Reese Park as is the Confederate statue. Both were moved from downtown because the streets became congested with cars.

Following this important July 4 celebration we went back home to our house on Harrold Avenue. My maternal grandparents joined us there, and we made a large freezer of peach ice cream; this was a special celebration in itself.

Leila and I had to do the churning. But we were well-rewarded by having an opportunity to lick the dasher when it was removed. Our parents were always generous in leaving a large amount of the dessert on the dasher. She had one side to consume and I the other. The freezer usually sat in its packed ice container for almost an hour in order to become very firm. Consequently, we were pleased to have a good taste of things to come. What could have been better on a hot, Georgia afternoon?

Here is Mother's recipe for that delicious treat. When peaches are plentiful, it might be a good plan for some of you to churn up a supply.

Mother's Homemade Peach Ice Cream

1 1/2 cups sugar
1/2 lemon, juiced
1 quart mashed, fresh, very ripe peaches
1 quart heavy cream
1 pint milk
1 teaspoon almond extract

Add sugar and lemon juice to mashed peaches. Mix cream, milk and flavoring, stirring until well blended. Combine with peach mixture; pour into freezer container.

Use freezer directions for filling with ice and freezer salt. Churn by hand until heavy and hard to move. Remove dasher and pack around container with ice. Allow to stand for 30 minutes to an hour in order to become very firm. Makes 2 1/2 quarts.

(Electric freezers are now available and work well with this recipe. But I must say that it was fun taking turns with my sister churning this delicacy.)

Sometimes Mama made this with a quart of boiled custard and eliminated the milk. The rest remained the same.

Swimming Hole

When I was a young child my father insisted that Leila and I learn to swim. Our mother had never learned and was afraid of deep water. She avoided it on all occasions, feeling that a bathtub was ample for holding the amount of wetness she desired.

Daddy had grown up on the old family plantation near Americus and learned to swim along with his brothers and playmates. They had a swimming hole made by damming up a little stream in their woods. They spent many happy, hot summer days playing in that spot.

Naturally, Daddy was eager for his daughters to have the same pleasure. He also felt it essential that we should learn to swim because he knew that we would be going to lake parties when we were older. It was not just the exercise or sport that he pushed, but the necessity of protecting ourselves.

Luckily there was a wide but shallow creek that we crossed en route to his farm. We often stopped there and just waded in the cool water on a hot day. Mother would join us.

It occurred to Daddy that he could shovel out a hole near the deepest part of the stream and make a little dam in order to provide a "swimming hole" for us. He contacted the owner of the acreage, who seemed pleased with the idea. Consequently the arrangements were made and our lessons began. As I recall, my older sister was already a swimmer, but I hadn't the slightest idea how to go about it.

There were two little swimming pools in the area, where she might have first learned. One was in Prospect Park, across town from our home on Harrold Avenue, and the other was Myrtle Springs, a recreation area out from town. The water in both was icy cold, and I hated it.

After preparing a deep area of the aforementioned stream, our creek swimming and my lessons began. Daddy would put his hands under my chest firmly and tell me to kick my feet and paddle or splash with my hands. He had a time getting me to put my chin in the water and insulted me once when he said that I looked just like a turtle paddling along with outstretched neck. This put determination into me, and I found that not struggling to keep my head so high made the job easier.

"This is only creek water, darling," he said to me. "If it gets into your face it won't hurt you and should it get in your mouth you can always spit it out." Such good advice was followed by his teaching me to do the "dead-man's" float. It came quite easily to lie face down with arms and legs extended and just drift. The pool was shallow enough for me to always touch bottom if I felt uneasy.

Once I'd learned that I could get my face completely wet and still survive, Daddy continued to work with my swimming. He began to hold onto me less firmly and eventually eased his hands away from my chest. Off I swam to my great surprise.

Cheers flew up from my sister and Mother. Leila would be swimming close by and Mom would be splashing her feet in the cool water. During peach season we would go out every Sunday afternoon for a swim before or after visiting the farm. Prior to the busy season, Daddy would take us to the swimming hole on hot days just for fun.

By the time I was eight or nine years old, a real swimming pool opened in Americus. It was complete with bath houses for boys and girls. There were sidewalks completely surrounding the pool. It had a roped-off area in the shallowest part for young children and a spring board for divers at the deepest end. In addition, there was a high dive, featuring two levels. I was sure that it was the height of a skyscraper, but its size has greatly diminished in my adult eyes.

We always had a family season ticket for each summer. It cost only $25.00. Imagine such a price. It gave us the opportunity of swimming as often as we liked. The same price applied to larger families than ours and if we had a visitor to accompany us we paid ten cents for their swim. There were many happy times for my family and friends at the pool, which still exists.

When we were small, Mother and our friend's moms would accompany us. They sat in a row of rocking chairs under a shelter next to the girls' bath house. All of them had large, palmetto fans and would create their own breezes as they watched the safety of their swimmers. They also dried and redressed us.

As we grew older and more accomplished, we were allowed to go alone. Leila would be with her friends and I with mine. We all looked out for each other. I remember once helping a little boy up to the side of the pool when he had gotten out too deep and couldn't swim. Another child noticed him and called to me, since I was nearby, to help. It was not a heroic effort on my part. The buoyancy of the water and smallness of the child made it quite simple to pull him to the edge and plop him up on the side of the pool.

I remember when I graduated from the roped-in area of the pool to the deeper part. All of my Hooks relatives were good swimmers and divers. They were almost always there too, and eager to help me learn their skills. I was never the greatest in this sport, but always adequate and still enjoy swimming from time to time.

My greatest accomplishment at the city pool was the day I finally mustered the courage to jump, not dive mind you, off that high, skyscraper structure. I climbed up to the top of the ladder and crept onto the platform. Looking down I could see my sister, Aunt Nancy, cousins Tommy and Margaret and Uncle Bobby, all Hookses, waiting in a circle to catch me if needed. After seeing this anxious group awaiting my triumph I dared not follow through. I held my nose and went off with a thud, bobbing up without a speck of help. How silly I felt to ever have been so frightened about such an easy venture.

Try your hand at these southern summer vegetable recipes.

Cook's Stewed Squash

2 cups chopped yellow squash
1 small onion, chopped
Salt and black pepper to taste
1 1/2 tablespoons bacon drippings or more if desired

In an iron skillet over medium heat, melt bacon drippings. Add vegetables and season. Stir from time to time to avoid sticking. When vegetables are thoroughly wilted serve at once with corn bread as a side dish.

Aunt Lily's Corn Salad

18 ears corn
6 bell peppers
6 sweet red peppers
6 large onions
2 bunches celery
Dry mustard to taste
1/2 cup salt
2 tablespoons tumeric
3 pounds sugar
2 quarts vinegar

Remove corn from cob. Add washed and chopped remaining vegetables. Mix in mustard, salt and tumeric, blending well. Add sugar and vinegar mixing thoroughly. Place over medium heat and cook, stirring from the bottom often to avoid sticking. When peppers turn brown remove from heat, pour into sterilized jars and seal. Makes a large quantity.

Always during the summer months our Americus churches sponsored large picnics. They were anticipated as soon as warm weather began. Once the announcement was made when specific groups were planning their annual event, the entire congregation became excited.

My maternal family, the Davenports, and my own family of four were all members of the First United Methodist Church. Daddy's Hooks relatives were all active at the First Baptist Church. Luckily for us we would have the opportunity of attending two of these gala events each summer.

The children would meet at the appointed church around 10 A.M. Our parents would take us there, but we were all delighted to board a high-sided truck that would take us to our destination. It was always Myrtle Springs, about six or seven miles from town.

This was not a hay-filled truck, for we stood holding on to the sides of the vehicle in order to see important places as we drove to the picnic. The entire little town of Americus would know when a group of this type might be cruising the streets of our town. The driver would blow the horn of the truck and we would be waving and yelling.

Just imagine a truckload of youngsters screaming at the top of their lungs. It was probably good that the noise was confined to a few times during the year. Store keepers would come out to wave to us in passing as did anyone whose home we drove by or persons walking down the streets. They all seemed to enjoy seeing us and wished to be included in our merriment.

Parents would drive out separately in order to be on hand for our arrival. They would carry along their best picnic foods, which the children knew would be served for them about noon. A tremendous ice box was placed on one end of the pavilion where the food would later be served on long tables.

After arrival, we would unload, find our parents and get our swimsuits, which they would have brought for us. The pool was very small and concrete with a deep end and diving board. The shallow section was too deep for tiny children. Instead, I recall a wooden platform with sides erected at the corner of the lowest portion to accommodate toddlers.

I absolutely hated that pool. It was filled with the coldest water God knew how to make. I was expected to take a swim because that was part of the day's program. After changing into my swimsuit in the little curtained bath house, I made a quick trip to the edges of the pool, jumped in and swam across. Then I was ready to get out, shivering as if I had tumbled full force into a snow bank. Other friends seemed to like the temperature of the springs. I was sometimes encouraged to swim a little longer by Leila or Martha, who must have been better adjusted to the coolness.

However, there were many fun things to do throughout the day. Martha was generally ready to accompany me to the long rope swings that hung from strong limbs of gigantic oak trees. There were also two sliding boards that we enjoyed, see-saws and a joggling board. We'd have to wait turns to use some of these pieces of equipment, but we could play hop scotch, jump rope or join in a game of dodge ball if one was in progress. Waiting turns was no bother.

Always the children would be anxious to call on Mr. Ott Johnson. He was an older man who made the lemonade for every church picnic that I ever attended. I don't recall his church affiliation, but it really didn't matter. Making this beverage seemed to be a specialty with him. He was always working at a spot a little distance from the pavilion.

We'd go to speak to him and watch him, a pleasant, bald man stirring the drink round and round with a sawed-off boat paddle. Sugar would have been poured into the bottom of the huge galvanized tub that was his choice of containers. Slices of fresh lemons floated around in swirls as he worked. He also squeezed extra lemons to add if needed. He was always pleasant to us and generous with samples if we had brought our own containers. All of this was before the days of paper cups and plates. Each family supplied their own tableware and even napkins or wash cloths.

Our mothers would sit on the pavilion benches or in chairs provided there and visit while we played. They were constantly on the sides of the pool if one of their youngsters was still swimming. I don't remember having lifeguards there, but older children and more advanced swimmers were called upon to look out for the younger ones.

Fathers would usually join us only for the noon meal since they could not leave their work too long. A large bell that hung on a pole was used to summon the group for our sumptuous picnic. Big boys in the group were allowed to pull the rope that rang it. The girls enjoyed watching their struggles.

Following what seemed an unending blessing of the food by the attending minister, the children were allowed to fill their plates first. I well remember one day when I had chosen three kinds of cake, two pieces of pie and chocolate fudge for my repast. When Mother saw it she made me share with the rest of our family and insisted that I should get a balanced meal.

I opted for baked ham in a small, hot biscuit, the "pully bone" of fried chicken, one deviled egg and half of a tomato sandwich. I was told to eat my salty foods first and could then have some of each of my choices of dessert. It seemed very unfair at the time, but now I can truly see her point.

Lemonade would be served from pitchers, and cookies, salted nuts, cheese straws, and some of the cakes would remain on the table, covered with netting to protect the food from insects. Treats were available throughout the afternoon, for those who chose to remain. I still wish that I could have a full plate of lemon cheese, chocolate layer, coconut, and devil's food cakes along with peach, pecan, apple, or blackberry pie. But I need to watch calories so perhaps it's just as well to remember these delicacies with such enthusiasm.

Blackberry Pie

1 quart blackberries, divided
Crusts for bottom and top of pie
3/4 cup sugar
2 tablespoons flour
1 tablespoon butter

Pick over, wash and drain berries. Prepare pastry by your favorite recipe or buy it prepared in the quantity needed. Line pan with pastry and place half of the berries in the bottom. Mix the sugar and flour and sprinkle over the berries. Add remaining half of fruit and cut butter into dots; place over berries then cover with top crust. Crimp edges of pastry. Make slits in the top crust to allow steam to be released while cooking. Bake at 350 degrees until top and edges of crust are brown. This makes a large pie and serves 10.

Divinity

3 cups sugar
1/2 cup white corn syrup
3/4 cup water
2 egg whites
1 teaspoon vanilla
1/2 teaspoon salt
1 cup chopped pecans

Combine sugar, syrup and water in saucepan; bring to a boil. Cover and let boil 3 minutes. (This avoids wiping crystals from pan sides.) Cook until small amount dropped into cold water forms a very firm ball. Pour slowly over egg whites to which vanilla and salt have been added. Beat together until moist peaks form when beater is withdrawn. Continue beating until mixture will almost hold its shape. Add nuts, drop by teaspoon on wax paper.

When we were in elementary school, we never considered playing with anyone a whole grade behind us—unless, of course, the person lived on Harrold Avenue, our special street. All ages came together there after school hours and during the summer when we played outside at night.

One of my lifelong friends, Elizabeth (Mathis) Cheatham fell into this category. She and her best childhood friend, Elizabeth Worthy, were almost as inseparable as my best friend Martha Marshall (Dykes) and I.

Thinking about her comes easy this time of year. Her birthday is Aug. 3, and I well remember a birthday party she had after moving onto our street. What could have been more appropriate than a watermelon cutting on a hot summer afternoon? That was our special treat.

Birthday party guests arrived barefoot and in play clothes. Our parents put us in play clothes, because they knew that we'd get melon juice on ourselves and that we would be playing active games. About midafternoon, Elizabeth's father, "Mr." Harvey, brought out several large melons for the cutting in the backyard, where tables had been set up.

Her mother, "Miss" Alice, gave us newspapers to spread on the table. We placed our melon slices on them to catch juice and seeds. When we finished, we folded the paper around the rind and tossed the debris into a nearby container.

We enjoyed shooting the slippery seeds through pinched fingers. We'd target someone in particular, in turn becoming the target of that person. When things got out of hand, parents would step in and stop it. Some of us would then see how far we could shoot the seeds.

We persuaded Mr. Harvey to cut small, thin sections of watermelon rinds. We'd carefully cut into the white part of the rim, making little squares all across the surface. We'd put the rinds in our mouths under the upper lip for fake "teeth." Some people made large or pointed teeth; others made dainty ones. It was hilarious to see each other with our melon rind dentures.

When I was very little, Mama or Daddy would make them for me and slide them under my lip, so I could blend in with the older children who'd come to visit my sister. It was hard to hold them in place and this added to our enjoyment. It was difficult to talk with watermelon rinds in our mouths. But we'd literally double over laughing at our weird-sounding words .

No special games were played at the birthday bash. But we climbed trees in her yard and enjoyed simple fun like hopscotch, jump rope and a toss-ball sport. Since the party included most kids on our street, it was a boy and girl fling. Some of Elizabeth's cousins and church friends attended as well. Later in the afternoon, the birthday cake was brought out to the yard tables, and we gathered around to sing "Happy Birthday" and enjoy the ice cream that was served with the cake.

During the summer months, many families cut watermelons for themselves. It was always a joyous occasion when our own Daddy did the cutting. He would thump the melon and declare that it was ripe enough to eat.

He was such a tease. It never failed for him to say, "It thumps fine, but look how green it is. I'm afraid it must be the same color on the inside too." This he did, especially if a new guest was on hand, for the rest of us knew his joke. After cutting the melon, he'd exclaim with genuine astonishment, "My goodness, it's just as red and ripe as it can be."

When the season is ripe for watermelon-seed spitting and shooting, I can't help but wonder if children still do this. My children did, and my daddy also pulled some of his same favorite tricks on them. But often after all the seeds were shot, cake eaten and guest s had gone home, the watermelon rinds were cleaned of their outer green surface and made into delicious pickles that we enjoyed throughout the year. A recipe for them follows.

Watermelon Rind Pickles

1/2 gallon of cut watermelon rind
3 tablespoons alum
2 pounds sugar
1/2 ounce whole cloves
1/2 ounce whole allspice
1 ounce whole mustard seed
1 quart apple cider vinegar

Cut the rind in small pieces, about 2-inch cubes. Pack in brine until ready to use. Put a layer of rinds and a layer of salt in a crock. Let stand until ready to make. Soak in clear water overnight or until they are fresh. Boil in 3 tablespoons alum added to water. Cook unti firm and brittle.

Boil again in plain water to remove the alum and the rinds are clear. Put sugar, spices and vinegar together; boil for 5 minutes. Add drained rinds and boil gently for 10 minutes.

Place pickles in jars and pour the hot vinegar over, having the jar full. Seal.

Fruit Salad Dressing

1/2 cup pineapple juice
1/4 cup orange juice
2 egg yolks, slightly beaten
3 tablespoons sugar
2 tablespoons flour
1 tablespoon butter
3/4 cup cream, whipped

Add juices to eggs and combine with mixed dry ingredients. Cook over hot water, strring constantly until mixture thickens. This will take about10 minutes. Add butter and cool. Fold in whipped cream. Chill well. Serve over fresh fruit and melon balls or any congealed fruit salad.

Exciting cowboy movies played every Saturday afternoon at the Rylander Theatre in Americus when I was growing up. On summer Saturdays, all of the children on our block of Harrold Avenue trooped there together. Each was admitted for a whole dime.

In addition to the featured film, we also had the advantage of a continuing serial show that was probably more thrilling to us than the main performance. I remember barely waiting from one Saturday to the next to see the next chapter.

I've no idea how many of these serials I saw from year to year, but I believe only a single one ran for several weeks each summer.

Particularly exciting was one titled "The Man Without a Head." With a name like that, no wonder I remember waiting for a week to see the next episode. And would you believe that I had to go on a two-week summer vacation and missed the very last chapter? Horrors! But my close friend Martha wrote and explained just who the headless man was. I hadn't even suspected him.

I don't know how the movie house was cooled, but the foyer was long and narrow with a tile floor. Because it was dark and large, I guess no sun ever really hit it. Air conditioning was not a part of that era, but I don't recall being overly hot there.

There were two aisles with rows of seats and boxes on each side of the center section in the main part of the movie house. The balcony was spacious; however, we sat there only when the theater was filled. There was what we called a "peanut" gallery above the entire rows of seats. To sit there cost only a nickel. If we hadn't the proper cash for the movie and a five-cent ice cream cone afterward, some of us might have tried this location. I recall only walking up there to see what it was like.

Our neighborhood group sat together in the center rows…sort of. Of course, the boys would be together, and the girls would be together in a different nearby section.

All of us anticipated seeing my great-aunt Lula Hooks Burkhalter arrive and plunk down in the front row. This meant it was time for the movie to begin, for she was always on time. Her white hair, under a smaller black-brimmed hat, seemed a strange appearance for a movie of this type. But she dearly loved the cowboys and also the "Pathe News" that was an additional feature of any movie there.

Originally all of our shows were black and white and without sound. Subtitles accompanied each scene; I think they must have helped our reading ability. Eventually both sound and color came for our pleasure.

A pianist played music during the entire afternoon. When the horses ran fast, she pounded on her piano. When a scene was extra exciting, she supplemented with a similar tune. Naturally, love or family scenes brought gentle melodies. It was a nice feature and we all knew the tiny little woman who offered such a nice sound background for our shows. When sound came to the movies, our musician no longer had a job with the theater, but she did teach music, I was told.

There were nearby drug stores where we stopped for our after-the-movie ice cream treats. I remember only three flavors chocolate, vanilla, and strawberry. We received one huge dip that was sort of pushed down into the flakey cone. These we licked all of the way back home as long as we could possibly make them last. Our trip was about seven or eight rather long blocks, but we had fun to and from our destination.

We always discussed the serial and the main show while walking home. The girls would comment on the actresses' clothes, and the boys were impressed with the males' heroic adventures. Of course, we tried to decide who the villain was in the serials and laughed at each others' remarks.

Aunt Lula lived on one of the streets on our route, and sometimes Martha and I would stop by and visit for a short time with her. We were still in awe that she, at her age and being rather dignified, so enjoyed cowboy shows. Because she knew that we liked the serials so very much, she would talk with us about them too, but I never had the feeling that she enjoyed them as much as we did.

I understand, from friends in my home town, that the Rylander has been renovated. It was really a grand movie house for a small town.

John Philip Sousa even came to town once when he was on a Southern tour and performed at this theatre. I was so little that Mama thought I should not go to the performance, but Daddy felt it was a once-in-a-lifetime experience, which it was. Since I was tiny I sat most of the time in his lap.

There were other minor stage shows to visit our town. Martha and I were particularly entranced with one called "The Sunset Kids." Little girls in fluffy dresses and swirling skirts tap danced for our entertainment. We were intrigued by their long blond, banana-type curls. We even pretended that we were one of them in the imaginary games we played, after explaining to each other just which one we'd chosen.

What pleasures this theater offered its residents and so did the following recipes.

Chicken Salad

1 fat hen or large-size fryer
1 large bunch of celery
1 cup homemade mayonnaise (see Note)
Salt and cayenne pepper to taste

Boil the hen until very tender. Remove from water and chill; pull from the bones, discarding all skin, gristle and veins. Cut with scissors in cubes about 1/2-inch or a little smaller. Add salt and pepper.

Clean celery and cut into small pieces about the same size as chicken. Mix together; add mayonnaise. Salad should have plenty of lemon juice in the mayonnaise and be seasoned well with salt and pepper. Mix thoroughly; chill before serving on crisp lettuce.

(Many people like to add hard boiled eggs and sweet pickle to this dish, but Mama never did. Naturally, I like hers the best.)

Note: If you are using commercial mayonnaise, add the juice of 1 lemon to the chicken and celery mixture before combining with dressing.) Serves 6 to 8 depending on size of chicken used.

Beet Salad

1 package lemon flavored gelatin
3/4 cup hot water
3/4 cup beet juice
1/2 cup vinegar
1 tablespoon prepared horseradish
1 cup chopped canned or cooked beets
1 cup chopped celery

Dissolve lemon flavored gelatin in hot water and beet juice. Add vinegar. When gelatin mixture thickens, add remaining ingredients and place in salad mold. Chill until firm. Serves 6 to 8.

Dress Up
For Summer Proms

During the summer months the young people in Americus enjoyed prom parties. I realize that these were popular in many Southern towns. But for those unfamiliar with them, I'd like to tell you about ours. The entertainments were in no way sophisticated events. We had junior and senior proms in high school, but even those in my day were not as elaborate as this generation's. Our neighborhood ones were simply organized get-togethers including both boys and girls. We were taught how to mix under great supervision, including a little formality. It was a gentle and fun lesson.

We must have been between the ages of eight and twelve years old when these events first started for us. Looking back on it now there are many things concerning them that seem ridiculous to me.

On our little Harrold Avenue, all the girls and boys played together daily. We were good friends and had not reached the age of dating. But the prom parties gave us an introduction to a more adult type of entertainment. During the mornings and afternoons we were barefoot and dressed for our usual summer games. But at party time, we were scrubbed clean and adorned in our Sunday clothes.

Girls had bows in their hair and special little nice pieces of jewelry to wear. We wanted to look special. The boys even wore ties, which I'm sure they hated. But this was part of the event.

We gathered at the host's home and went to the houses with neighbors or alone. We knew everybody on the street so well it was simply a matter of getting ourselves to the proper place on time. Should a party be in a different neighborhood, our parents would drive us to our destination and return in time to retrieve us.

Once we arrived the guests were all properly greeted. If visitors were present, they were quickly introduced. After admiring each others' dressed-up outfits or just talking with the group, all were given darling little prom cards. They had numbered lines and a tiny pencil attached at the top with a cord. On the cover there was always a delightful colored picture, appropriate for the occasion. These were required in order to write the names of those with whom we would prom in the sequence of listing. Those minute pencils were about the size of a birthday candle and we treasured them even after a party had ended.

Boys politely asked girls for proms. We were terrified that our card may not be filled and we'd feel very unpopular if that happened. But realizing now how carefully our hosts supervised us, I'm sure that nobody was ever left out. After filling the cards, a bell would ring to announce the first prom. This simply meant a walk around one block or we might stop in somebody's yard to talk with a group. Sometimes we'd even go in pairs.

There were also a few yard swings of which we took advantage. The boy would push the girl in the swaying seat, which was far from what might have been in his mind during earlier day's play. But this was expected of them and they responded with nice manners.

Proms were timed and the bell would ring loudly when alloted moments designated for the short walk concluded. I believe that they usually lasted about ten or maybe fifteen minutes. There were only about ten proms during a party.

We would regroup at the host's house, usually on the front porch. Punch or lemonade was always ready for us throughout the evening. Assorted homemade cookies, roasted pecans or peanuts and cheese straws were served. After enjoying a taste of the refreshments, our next person on the prom card would come forward for the arranged stroll.

Each of us was very conscientious about returning from our walks on time. I remember one night when some children from other parts of the town had joined us. They were classmates or Sunday School friends or maybe cousins. I was delighted that my favorite boy at the time, Billy Smith, had been invited to one of these parties.

Fortunately he had asked me for one prom, which was joy to my soul. We had decided to take advantage of a seesaw in a neighbor's yard for our prom. When the bell rang, he was up in the air at the end of the board and I jumped off the down part in such a hurry that he slammed to the ground. It was very embarrassing, but I explained that the bell had rung and I knew we had to hurry back.

"You might have eased me down," he said, and right he was.

Fortunately, it didn't seem to spoil our fondness for each other and we even had an additional stroll that same evening. I still consider him to be one of my very best friends.

There was another time when I was walking swiftly around the block with Clarke Pool, one of my street neighbors with whom I played constantly. We walked so fast that my feet hurt and he said that his did, too. We sat right down and took off our shoes and socks and returned to the party barefoot. But why not? We weren't used to wearing our Sunday shoes for such fast stepping.

When we returned, the immediate instructions were to put the footwear back on before starting out again. The hostess seemed amused at the sight of us. She told us to walk more slowly and not so far the next time.

These little events usually began in the early evening and we were all safely home by bedtime.

I remember saving my prom cards, as did the other girls. The next day we would discuss our partners and the entire event. We kept many of these as souvenirs for years. I particularly liked the tiny pencils and kept them in a collection.

The proms brought boys and girls together on a basis different than our daily climbing trees or playing ball. It just seemed proper to be well dressed for these occasions after spending daytime hours in our grubby play clothes. We always enjoyed the simple refreshments served. The next two are typical.

Americus Cheese Straws

1 pound New York extra-sharp cheese
3/4 cup vegetable oil
1 teaspoon salt
1/4 teaspoon soda
4 cups flour
Cayenne pepper to taste

Grate cheese and mix with oil by hand. Add other ingredients that have been previously combined. Roll out about 1/4-inch thick on floured board and cut with cheese straw wheel or put through a cookie press. Bake at 350 degrees for 10 to 15 minutes or until crisp. Makes a large quantity.

Peach Cookies

2 1/4 cups plain flour
1 teaspoon baking powder
1/2 teaspoon soda
1/2 teaspoon salt
3/4 cup vegetable shortening
1 cup sugar
2 eggs
2 tablespoons milk
1 teaspoon almond flavoring
1 cup chopped pecans
1 cup finely chopped or mashed peaches
Crushed corn flakes

Sift dry ingredients together and set aside. Combine shortening, sugar and eggs, blending well. Add milk and flavoring. Blend in dry ingredients and finally add pecans and peaches. Shape dough into balls, teaspoon size, and roll in crushed corn flakes. Bake at 375 degrees for 10 to 12 minutes. Do not stack until cool.

Saturday Cowboy Movies

I wrote about how much the children in my neighborhood enjoyed going to the movies together. Now I should like to tell you about some of the fun that followed during the week after our cinema entertainment.

The older children in our block would seriously select character parts among themselves and re-act the past Saturday's performance. Since I was one of the younger ones at this point in my life, I would go to see what they were doing. I was among other siblings who followed brothers or sisters to the place of entertainment. We sat on benches as the show progressed and served as the audience.

Leila was extremely popular with her age group. She would almost always have a part in the play, and I was so proud of her. Tom Harris, the roughest boy in the neighborhood but a nice kid, was always the villain by choice. There were several big boys, about the same age, and they would take turns being the "good" guy. My sister was often the heroine, but shared honors with other girls her age. These so-called actors would take minor or major parts as the group desired. There never seemed to be disagreement about this. It was sort of understood that leads should be shared with the exception of the villain.

Broomsticks were used for horses, since most of our Saturday movies were cowboy ones. All of the boys had cowboy hats and bandannas, and it was easy for them to get some rope for lassos. The girls would borrow appropriate clothing from their mothers to be correctly dressed as possible for each scene. Props also were gathered and placed appropriately.

Younger siblings would be sent home to fetch what was needed to make the show seem real. This gave us a feeling of importance as well as acceptance. In my mind's eye I can see some of those older girls wobbling in their moms' high heels, draped in scarves or satin sashes.

Sometimes it would take an entire morning and part of the afternoon to have everything placed and ready for the performance. Then the action would begin, and it was a fun-filled time.

One day it was necessary for the villain to be bound to a tree to be burned for his misdeeds. Some suggested coloring flames on paper and putting them on top of a pile of wood to represent the fire. The scene definitely had to be authentic for it was the most important portion of the entire show. The audience, or background workers, picked up twigs to place under the colorful flames.

Our brave villain said that paper flames did not look real enough and suggested that a few matches could be lighted and placed together far enough under his bare feet, but not close enough to hurt. It was a much better idea than crayon colored flames. Our sticks were tossed aside and the matches immediately secured.

Tom was promptly tied to the tree. Everyone was tense as the "good" people acted their parts. When the matches were ignited, somehow a large piece of paper fell onto the small flames. The discarded twigs caught fire and a blaze was glowing in the McKlesky's backyard. The villain was immediately released, but fell into the edge of the blaze and singed his eyebrows.

We made no effort to smother the flames. Getting our brave, mean guy off the tree was more important. Most of us were terrified. Even the grass around the area caught fire. The parents in the house where we were playing called a firetruck. When we heard the sirens, there was a complete scattering. Most of the children were large enough to climb over the back or side fence, depending on which part of the block our houses were located. We headed for home in no time flat. We didn't want the firemen to think that any of us had a thing to do with this combustion.

I was too little to get over the fence. My sister and our next-door neighbor, who was almost like a brother, came back for my rescue and boosted me over after they had already begun to run up the alley that ran behind all of our homes. They pulled me up so fast that the buttons popped off the back of my dress. "Run as fast as you can" was almost a chorus.

By this time, the firetruck had entered the back yard where we had been playing. We could see it well, but hoped nobody saw us, as though it was a puzzle to wonder just who had been playing there all day long.

Actually no harm was done to the property. But all of us were called together in one spot. A parent from each family was present. We were emphatically reprimanded for our misdeed. We were cautioned about the dangers that might have been involved. It was a good lesson. I can never forget that fire and the horrors that might have evolved.

Nobody ever knew how that big piece of paper found its way to the lighted matches below our villain's feet. Much discussion naturally took place. Some thought the paper was deliberately planted by the next-to-roughest boy in our group who was probably jealous of the chosen one. It was never established, but my sister's group whispered about it for a long time to come.

Enjoy the recipes.

Fairy Cones

6 egg yolks
3 level tablespoons sugar
2 level tablespoons flour
1 cup chopped pecans or English walnuts
Whipped cream, sweetened and flavored or ice cream

Beat the egg yolks with sugar. Add flour then the nuts and spread as thinly as possible on greased, flat baking sheets. Bake about 7 minutes at 375 degrees. While still warm, cut into squares and roll each in the form of a cone. Store in air-tight containers. When needed, fill with cream or ice cream.

Marguerites

Desired number of saltine crackers
Same number of large size marshmallows

Place marshmallow in center of cracker. Put on ungreased cookie sheet and place in hot, preheated oven, 375 degrees. Cook until marshmallow melts over top of cracker and is lightly brown. This is a quick treat for a group of unexpected, young children.

Index of Recipes

Colophon

Remember When…?
Family, Friends, and Recipes
By Clara Belle Hooks Eschmann
Published by Mercer University Press
October 1998
Book Design by Jay Polk
Book Jacket Design by Jim Burt
Black and White Illustrations by Barclay Burns
Cover Illustration: "Papaw's Favorites" by Susan B. Jolley
Text font: Adobe® Garamond
Book Jacket printed by Phoenix Color
Book printing by Edwards Brothers